200 Air Fryer Recipes

hamlyn | **all colour cookbook**

200 Air Fryer Recipes

Denise Smart

hamlyn

First published in Great Britain in
2023 by Hamlyn,
an imprint of Octopus Publishing
Group Ltd
Carmelite House
50 Victoria Embankment
London EC4Y 0DZ
www.octopusbooks.co.uk

An Hachette UK Company
www.hachette.co.uk

Distributed in the US by
Hachette Book Group
1290 Avenue of the Americas
4th and 5th Floors
New York, NY 10104

Distributed in Canada by
Canadian Manda Group
664 Annette St., Toronto,
Ontario, Canada M6S 2C8

Denise Smart asserts the moral
right to be identified as the author
of this work.

ISBN 978-0-600-63811-7

A CIP catalogue record for this book
is available from the British Library.

Printed and bound in China.

10 9 8 7 6 5 4 3 2 1

MIX
Paper | Supporting
responsible forestry
FSC
www.fsc.org
FSC® C144853

Standard level spoon measurement
are used in all recipes.
1 tablespoon = one 15 ml spoon
1 teaspoon = one 5 ml spoon

Both imperial and metric
measurements have been given
in all recipes. Use one set of
measurements only and not
a mixture of both.

Eggs should be medium unless
otherwise stated. The Department
of Health advises that eggs should
not be consumed raw. This book
contains dishes made with raw or
lightly cooked eggs. It is prudent
for more vulnerable people such
as pregnant and nursing mothers,
invalids, the elderly, babies and
young children to avoid uncooked
or lightly cooked dishes made with
eggs. Once prepared these dishes
should be kept refrigerated and
used promptly.

Milk should be full fat unless
otherwise stated.

Fresh herbs should be used unless
otherwise stated. If unavailable use
dried herbs as an alternative but
halve the quantities stated.

Pepper should be freshly ground
black pepper unless otherwise stated.

This book includes dishes made
with nuts and nut derivatives. It
is advisable for those with known
allergic reactions to nuts and nut
derivatives and those who may
be potentially vulnerable to these
allergies to avoid dishes made with
nuts and nut oils. It is also prudent
to check the labels of pre-prepared
ingredients for the possible inclusion
of nut derivatives.

contents

introduction

introduction

If you've purchased this book, you are probably already the proud owner of an air fryer – the must-have kitchen appliance that everyone is talking about.

This book will show you exactly why air fryers have become so popular. Rest assured, this is not just another impulsive purchase that you will eventually tire of and pack away in the back of a cupboard. Affordable, energy-efficient and easy, air fryers can revolutionize your kitchen experience. These handy gadgets use less energy and oil and take less time than conventional ovens, helping you prepare fuss-free versions of all your favourite dishes.

Whether you are a beginner, or an experienced air fryer user seeking fresh inspiration, this cookbook will show you how to get the most out of this amazing appliance.

The book contains 200 easy-to-prepare sweet and savoury dishes, suitable for every occasion. All of the recipes use easily sourced ingredients and are guaranteed to make the process of preparing and cooking food in your air fryer simple and successful. In this book, you will find delicious ideas for breakfast, quick snacks, light bites, vegetarian and vegan meals, meat and fish mains, sides and sweet treats.

what is an air fryer?
An air fryer is basically a small oven. The name is deceptive because it is not a traditional 'fryer' as we know it, but it cooks food in a way that achieves that same fried effect.

Air fryers contain a heating element located at the top which is enhanced by a powerful fan. The fan circulates the hot air around the food, which sits on a removable crisping plate. Air fryers typically heat up and cook food very quickly and evenly, thanks to the concentrated heat source as well as the size and position of the fan. Because of their well-balanced time and temperature controls, air fryers produce perfect food that is juicy, crispy and delicious.

which is the best air fryer for me?
There are many air fryers on the market – the range can be mind-boggling for the first-time buyer. However, there are several factors that are worth considering to help you narrow down your selection.

First, take into account the different functions. Many air fryers have pre-set programmes for meat, fish, vegetables and frozen foods. Some models have a 'shake' function, which reminds you to shake the basket or turn the food halfway through the cooking time. Others have a 'keep warm' function. Some air fryers have a single drawer, while others have dual drawers that allow you to cook different foods at different temperatures at the same time, or cook a main and a side simultaneously. Consider which features and functions are most appealing for your household.

The second factor to take into consideration is how many people you are cooking for as different air fryers have different capacities. The smallest air fryers (1–2 litres/quarts in volume) are suitable for 1–2 people, the medium sizes (3–4 litres/quarts in volume) are good for 2–3 people, and the largest air fryers (6 litres/quarts or more in volume) are perfect if you are cooking for 4–6 people.

Finally, you need to take note of how much room you have in your kitchen, as some models can take up a lot of worktop space.

The recipes in this book were prepared in a 5 litre (5 quart) air fryer with a single drawer. This is big enough to accommodate four pieces of fish or chicken breasts, a whole 1.5 kg (3 lb) chicken or an 18–20 cm (7–8 inch) round tin or ovenproof dish.

what are the benefits of an air fryer?

Air fryers are much healthier Traditional frying methods use lots of oil. However, with an air fryer, you can make foods like chips, goujons and doughnuts with only 1–2 teaspoons of oil.

Air fryers are energy efficient Because they are smaller than conventional ovens, air fryers heat up quicker and cook food faster, which could save you money on your electricity bills.

Air fryers are quicker Although you may occasionally need to cook in batches (depending on the size of your appliance), overall, having an air fryer will save you time in the kitchen. In general, air fryers reduce cooking times by about 20 per cent.

Air fryers are perfect for small-batch bakes Because of their size, these appliances lend themselves well to baking small batches of cakes, cookies and other sweet treats.

Air fryers are great for reheating Whereas microwaving can make certain foods go soggy, air fryers allow you to reheat your meals and still retain that delicious, crispy crunch.

Air fryers are amazing for cooking frozen foods Conventional ovens can often dry out frozen foods but air fryers are perfect for cooking frozen chips, potato wedges and fish fingers.

Air fryers are fuss-free appliances Unlike traditional ovens, an air fryer will not heat up your whole kitchen, and it will lessen the intensity of cooking smells. Using an air fryer also means you have minimal clean up at the end.

Air fryers are especially good for meat and fish Cooking times can be a bit of a guessing game on the hob or in the oven, but air fryers allow you to achieve deliciously juicy meat and fish dishes more easily and reduce the risk of drying out your food.

do I need any special equipment?
The simple answer is no, but you might consider using the following equipment to make your air frying experience even easier:

- Small metal baking tins, 17 cm (6½ inches) square and up to 20 cm (8 inches) round, depending on the size of your air fryer.

- Small ovenproof dishes, ramekins and small metal pudding tins.

- Spray bottles for oil. Some of the recipes in this book recommend spritzing your food with oil to make it crispy.

- Pastry brush, for brushing oil and glazing the surfaces of food.

- Perforated silicone liners or mats for air fryers. Alternatively, you can simply pierce holes in pieces of nonstick baking paper, although remember never to place these in your air fryer without any food on top as they could fly into the fan element and catch fire.

- Rubber-tipped heatproof tongs, for turning food. These also prevent you from scratching the tray.

- Foil, for covering food. This prevents food with longer cooking times from becoming too brown.

- Mandolin, for making evenly sized, thin slices of fruits and vegetables.

- Small metal, wooden or bamboo skewers that fit in your air fryer. If you are using wood or bamboo, remember to soak them in water first to prevent burning.

- Thermometer. This is not essential, but it is useful for checking that chicken and larger cuts of meat are cooked through.

tips for using your air fryer

- Always read the manufacturer's instructions before using your new air fryer. This will help you operate your appliance properly and safely and ensure you get the best results.

- The recipes in this book specify standard oven cooking temperatures. Some air fryers come with less standard temperatures, so just choose the closest setting to the temperature specified. For example, your air fryer may have 199°C (390°F) instead of 200°C (400°F). Like ovens, different models might cook slightly hotter or cooler. This means you may have to adjust the cooking time by a minute or so. Be mindful of any slight variation on your own model.

- Most of the recipes in this book recommend shaking or turning the food partway through cooking for an even cook. The benefit of the air fryer is that you can open the drawer and check the food without all the heat escaping, especially during the last few minutes.

- Preheating your air fryer to the temperature recommended will reduce cooking times.

- Cut vegetables and meat into even-sized pieces so they cook at the same rate.

- When cooking large joints of meat, you may need to remove the plate and sit the meat in the bottom of your air fryer for roasting.

- Always cook food in a single layer. Never overcrowd the drawer, or your food will cook unevenly and take longer. Air fryers work by circulating air around food, so require space.

- You will still require a little oil to cook most foods, especially breaded foods, so consider filling a small spray bottle with oil to help you achieve that perfect, crispy crumb.

- Cover dishes with foil to prevent the food from becoming too brown. This is especially useful for larger cakes and quiches.

- Clean your appliance after every use. Air fryers are easy to clean with hot soapy water.

- Never fill your appliance with oil – it is not a deep fryer.

the best foods for air frying

Potatoes – chips (homemade or frozen), whole baked potatoes, wedges, roast

Meat – steak, chicken, lamb chops, pork chops, bacon rashers

Fish – salmon fillets, cod fillets, prawns

Vegetables – cauliflower, carrots, parsnips, courgettes, peppers, aubergines

Pastry – shortcrust, puff, filo

Fruit – stone fruits (such as peaches and apricots), pineapple, apples, bananas

foods to avoid
Uncoated popcorn or popcorn kernels – they may fly into the element and cause damage

Wet, saucy foods – foods with lots of sauce, such as stews, or foods coated in drippy batter don't cook well in an air fryer. Dry spice rubs, glazes and dried breadcrumbs work best

Rice, pasta and pulses – dry foods that need to soften as they boil in water should not be cooked in an air fryer

store cupboard and freezer essentials
Below are some of the most commonly used ingredients in the recipes:

- Oils – olive oil, sunflower oil and flavoured oils, such as chilli and garlic

- Dried breadcrumbs – fine and panko

- Dried herbs – mixed herbs, oregano, rosemary and thyme

- Dried garlic and onion powder

- Spices – paprika, ground cinnamon, ginger, cumin and chilli

- Ready-prepared spice mixes – Moroccan, Middle Eastern, piri piri and Mexican

- Pastes – harissa, pesto, tikka, gochujang, miso and chipotle

- Nuts – almonds, walnuts, pistachios and pine nuts

- Dried fruits – apricots, mixed berries, mixed tropical fruit and dates

- Seeds – sesame, pumpkin, sunflower and linseed

- Flours – plain, self-raising, cornflour and baking powder

- Sugars – caster, granulated, soft brown, honey and maple syrup

- Sauces – sweet chilli, ketchup, sriracha, piri piri and soy sauce

- Frozen foods – peas, fish fingers, frozen chips and fries

it's time to get cooking!

The recipes in this book will inspire you to get creative – whether it's for one, two, or for the whole family – so get started by picking one of the delicious choices and giving it a try. It's amazing what you can create with fresh vegetables and store cupboard ingredients and, as air frying is a healthier way of cooking, you will be able to enjoy well-balanced meals in a fraction of the time.

The more you cook with it, the more you will discover inventive ways to use your air fryer. Remember, because it's portable, this appliance can also be used away from home on staycations.

Like many air fryer owners, you will soon find that you can't wait to tell your friends and family about all the tasty dishes you've created from just a few simple ingredients.

Happy air frying!

breakfast

apricot & almond pastries

Makes **6**
Preparation time **15 minutes**
Cooking time **20 minutes**

125 g (4 oz) **mascarpone cheese**
25 g (1 oz) **icing sugar**
50 g (2 oz) **ground almonds**
½ teaspoon **almond extract**
1 sheet of **ready-rolled puff pastry**
beaten **egg**, to glaze
6 **apricot halves**, fresh or from a can, drained
25 g (1 oz) **flaked almonds**
2 tablespoons **apricot jam**

Place the mascarpone, icing sugar, ground almonds and almond extract in a bowl and mix well.

Unroll the puff pastry and cut it into 6 squares, about 10 cm (4 inches) across. Divide the almond mixture equally between the squares, spreading it out slightly but leaving a 1 cm (½ inch) border on all sides. Brush the edges of the pastry with a little beaten egg, then lift 2 opposite corners of one of the pastries and pinch together, before repeating with the other 2 corners, to make a parcel.

Push down in the centre of the parcel to make a well and pop an apricot half on top. Repeat with the remaining pastries. Brush the pastries with egg and sprinkle over the flaked almonds.

Cook half the pastries in a preheated air fryer at 180°C (350°F) for 9–10 minutes, until risen and golden and the bases are crispy. Repeat with the remaining pastries.

Warm the jam, then brush over the tops of the pastries to glaze. Serve warm or cold.

For cherry & almond Danish pastries, prepare the mascarpone filling as above. Cut the pastry into 6 squares as above, then score a 1 cm (½ inch) border around the edges of each pastry. Divide the filling between the pastries and spread within the border, then scatter with 200 g (7 oz) of halved pitted cherries. Brush around the edges of the pastry with a little beaten egg and sprinkle over the flaked almonds, then cook in batches as above, until crisp. Dust with a little icing sugar.

buckwheat & tropical fruit muesli

Serves **4**

Preparation time **5 minutes, plus cooling**

Cooking time **15 minutes**

150 g (5 oz) **buckwheat**

50 g (2 oz) **porridge oats**

25 g (1 oz) **chia seeds**

2 tablespoons **mixed seeds**, such as pumpkin, sunflower and linseed

2 tablespoons melted **coconut oil**

1 teaspoon **ground ginger**

1 tablespoon **agave** or **maple syrup**

125 g (4 oz) **dried mixed tropical fruit**, such as pineapple, mango and papaya, chopped

50 g (2 oz) **dried toasted coconut flakes** or **shavings**

milk or **yogurt**, to serve

Mix all the ingredients, except the dried fruit and coconut, in a large bowl until well combined.

Spread the muesli over a piece of pierced nonstick baking paper in a preheated air fryer and cook at 150°C (300°F) for 13–15 minutes, until golden, stirring once.

Remove from the air fryer and allow to cool. Stir in the dried fruit and coconut and store in an airtight container for up to 4 weeks. Serve with milk or yogurt.

For buckwheat, chocolate & almond muesli, prepare the muesli as above, substituting the ground ginger with 50 g (2 oz) of chopped almonds and 1 teaspoon of vanilla extract. Cook as above. When cool, replace the dried fruit and coconut flakes with 50 g (2 oz) of dark chocolate chunks.

banana breakfast loaf

Serves **4–6**
Preparation time **10 minutes**
Cooking time **30 minutes**

3 tablespoons **olive** or
  sunflower oil, plus extra
  for greasing
2 tablespoons **honey**
1 **egg**, beaten
2 ripe **bananas**, mashed
3 tablespoons **buttermilk** or
  natural yogurt
75 g (3 oz) **plain flour**
75 g (3 oz) **spelt** or
  wholemeal flour
½ teaspoon **bicarbonate
  of soda**
½ teaspoon **baking powder**
1 teaspoon **ground mixed
  spice**
1 tablespoon **chia seeds**
50 g (2 oz) **pitted dates**,
  chopped
50 g (2 oz) **pecans**, roughly
  chopped

To serve
natural yogurt
mixed berries, such as
  raspberries or blueberries

Grease and line the base of a 500 g (1 lb) loaf tin or an 18 cm (7 inch) round cake tin, 7 cm (3 inches) deep, with nonstick baking paper.

Whisk together the oil, honey, egg, bananas and buttermilk in a large bowl. Sift over the flours, bicarbonate of soda, baking powder and mixed spice. Stir until combined, then stir in the chia seeds, dates and pecans, until well combined. Spoon into the prepared tin.

Cook in a preheated air fryer at 150°C (300°F) for 30 minutes, until golden brown and risen and a skewer inserted into the middle comes out clean.

Cool in the tin for a few minutes, then turn out on to a wire rack to cool completely before serving in slices with yogurt and fresh berries.

For chocolate & banana bread, make the banana bread as above, using 50 g (2 oz) of plain flour and 25 g (1 oz) of cocoa powder instead of 75 g (3 oz) of plain flour. Substitute the pecans and dates with 50 g (2 oz) of chopped Brazil nuts and 75 g (3 oz) of dark chocolate chunks. Cook as above.

sweet potato & chorizo hash

Serves **2**
Preparation time **10 minutes**
Cooking time **20 minutes**

500 g (1 lb) **sweet potatoes**,
   peeled and cut into 2.5 cm
   (1 inch) pieces
1 teaspoon **sunflower oil**
2 small **red onions**, cut into
   wedges
200 g (7 oz) **cooking chorizo**,
   cut into chunks
2 **eggs**
salt and **pepper**

Smashed avocado
1 **avocado**
juice of ½ **lime**
3 drops of **hot pepper sauce**

Toss the sweet potato chunks with the oil and season with a little salt and pepper. Cook in a preheated air fryer at 180°C (350°F) for 10 minutes, stirring once.

Add the onions and chorizo and stir to mix. Cook for 4 minutes, stir again and add the eggs in their shells. Cook for a further 6 minutes, or until the chorizo and potatoes start to crisp. Remove the eggs after 6 minutes if you want the yolks runny.

Meanwhile, cut the avocado in half, remove the stone and scoop the flesh into a bowl. Add the lime juice, hot pepper sauce and some salt. Using the back of a spoon, roughly smash the avocado until still slightly chunky.

Divide the hash between 2 plates. Peel the eggs, cut in half and place on top of the hash. Serve with the smashed avocado, drizzled with a little chorizo oil from the bottom of the air fryer.

For sweet potato & chorizo breakfast burrito, prepare and cook the sweet potatoes, onions and chorizo as above. While it's cooking, prepare the smashed avocado and warm 2 flour tortillas. Divide the hash between the warmed tortillas, add 1 tablespoon of ready-made tomato salsa, the smashed avocado and a little chopped fresh coriander. Fold the tortillas and serve immediately.

shakshuka with feta

Serves **2**
Preparation time **5 minutes**
Cooking time **16 minutes**

1 **red onion**, sliced
1 small **red pepper**, cored,
   deseeded and thinly sliced
2 teaspoons **olive oil**
¼ teaspoon **smoked chilli**
   flakes
50 g (2 oz) **feta cheese**,
   crumbled
2 **eggs**
1 tablespoon chopped **flat**
   leaf parsley
pepper
crusty bread, to serve

Tomato sauce
250 g (8 oz) canned **chopped**
   tomatoes
1 tablespoon **tomato ketchup**
1 **garlic clove**, crushed
½ teaspoon **ground cumin**
½ teaspoon **ground coriander**
½ teaspoon **smoked hot**
   paprika
salt and **pepper**

Place the onion, red pepper, olive oil and chilli flakes in an ovenproof dish or tin. Stir well, place the dish in a preheated air fryer and cook at 180°C (350°F) for 10 minutes, stirring halfway through.

Meanwhile, combine all the sauce ingredients together in a bowl. When the vegetables have finished cooking, pour over the sauce and stir well.

Stir in half the feta, then make 2 wells in the mixture and crack in the eggs. Return to the air fryer and cook for a further 5–6 minutes, or until the eggs are just set.

Sprinkle over the remaining feta, parsley and pepper. Serve immediately with crusty bread.

For baked eggs with ham, spinach & cheese, brush 2 ramekins with a little oil and line each ramekin with a slice of ham. Place 50 g (2 oz) of baby spinach leaves in a colander and pour over boiling water to wilt it. Drain well and when cool enough to handle, squeeze out the excess water. Divide the spinach between the ramekins, then sprinkle over 25 g (1 oz) of grated Cheddar cheese. Crack an egg into each ham case, sprinkle with a little more cheese and a little paprika, then place the ramekins in a preheated air fryer and cook at 180°C (350°F) for 5–7 minutes, or until the eggs are just set.

all day breakfast

Serves **1**
Preparation time **2 minutes**
Cooking time **14 minutes**

1 **sausage**
2 **back bacon rashers**
1 large **flat** or **Portobello**
   mushroom, thickly sliced
1 **tomato**, halved
sunflower oil, for spritzing
   and brushing
1 **egg**
salt and **pepper**

To serve
buttered toast
ketchup or **brown sauce**

Cook the sausage in a preheated air fryer at 180°C
(350°F) for 6 minutes, then turn the sausage and add
the bacon, mushroom and tomato halves. Spritz the
mushroom slices with a little oil and cook for a further
4 minutes.

Turn the bacon and mushrooms, then brush a small
ramekin with oil, break in the egg and add to the air
fryer. Cook for a further 4 minutes, until the egg white
is set but the yolk still runny. The bacon will be crispy
and the sausage cooked through.

Season to taste and serve immediately with hot
buttered toast and sauce of your choice.

For veggie all day breakfast, cut 4 new potatoes into
1.5 cm (¾ inch) pieces, toss in 1 teaspoon of sunflower
oil and season with salt and pepper. Cook in a preheated
air fryer at 180°C (350°F) for 8 minutes, then turn the
potatoes. Add 2 vegetarian sausages, the tomato halves
and the sliced mushrooms, spritzed with a little oil. Cook
for a further 4 minutes, then turn the mushrooms and
sausages. Prepare a ramekin as above and crack in an
egg. Cook for a further 4–5 minutes, until the egg is set
and the potatoes crispy.

brioche cinnamon french toast

Serves **2**
Preparation time **5 minutes**
Cooking time **8 minutes**

1 large **egg**
½ teaspoon **ground cinnamon**
1 tablespoon **caster sugar**
50 ml (2 fl oz) **milk**
2 thick slices of **brioche**
sunflower oil, for spritzing
maple syrup, to drizzle

Whisk together the egg, cinnamon and sugar in a shallow bowl, then whisk in the milk. Add the slices of brioche, leave for a few minutes to soak up some of the mixture, then turn over and leave until all the egg mixture has been absorbed.

Place the bread in a preheated air fryer, spritz with a little oil and cook at 200°C (400°F) for 4 minutes. Turn over and cook for a further 3–4 minutes, until golden. Serve immediately, drizzled with maple syrup.

For caramelized banana, to serve as an accompaniment, cut a banana in half lengthways and sprinkle with 1 tablespoon of light soft brown sugar to coat. Cook on a piece of pierced nonstick baking paper in a preheated air fryer at 190°C (375°F) for 6–7 minutes. Serve with your prepared French toast.

fruity granola

Serves **4**

Preparation time **5 minutes,
plus cooling**

Cooking time **25 minutes**

3 tablespoons **maple syrup**
or **honey**

1 tablespoon **sunflower oil**

200 g (7 oz) **porridge oats**

50 g (2 oz) **pecans**, roughly
chopped

50 g (2 oz) **almonds**, roughly
chopped

100 g (3½ oz) **mixed seeds**,
such as sunflower, pumpkin
and linseed

1 teaspoon **ground cinnamon**

100 g (3½ oz) **dried mixed
berries**, such as blueberries,
cranberries, strawberries
and cherries

To serve
milk or **yogurt**
fresh **blueberries**

Heat the maple syrup and oil in a small saucepan over
a gentle heat. Place the oats, nuts, seeds and cinnamon
in a large bowl and mix well. Pour over the warm maple
syrup mixture and stir well to combine.

Spread the granola over a piece of pierced nonstick
baking paper in a preheated air fryer and cook at 150°C
(300°F) for 20–25 minutes, stirring once, until golden.

Remove the granola from the air fryer and allow to
cool. Stir in the dried berries and store in an airtight
container for up to 4 weeks. Serve with milk or yogurt
and fresh blueberries.

For chocolate & nut trail mix, combine 50 g (2 oz) each
of walnuts, hazelnuts and almonds in a large bowl with
25 g (1 oz) of coconut flakes. Pour over 1 tablespoon of
sunflower oil, 1 tablespoon of maple syrup, ½ teaspoon
of vanilla extract and ½ teaspoon of salt and stir well.
Spread over a piece of pierced nonstick baking paper
in a preheated air fryer and cook at 160°C (325°F) for
6 minutes, until golden and crisp. Allow to cool, then stir
in 50 g (2 oz) each of dark chocolate chunks and raisins.

bacon butties with smoky ketchup

Serves **2**

Preparation time **5 minutes,
    plus cooling**

Cooking time **23 minutes**

4 **back bacon rashers**
butter, for spreading
4 slices of **white bread**

Smoky ketchup
4 **plum tomatoes**, about 350 g
    (11½ oz), quartered
1 small **onion**, roughly chopped
2 teaspoons **smoked paprika**
1 teaspoon **olive oil**
2 teaspoons **cider** or **white
    wine vinegar**
2 teaspoons **light soft brown
    sugar**
2 teaspoons **Worcestershire
    sauce**
2 teaspoons **tomato purée**
salt and **pepper**

Make the ketchup. Place the tomatoes, onion, paprika, oil, vinegar, salt and pepper in an ovenproof dish. Stir well, place the dish in a preheated air fryer and cook at 180°C (350°F) for 15 minutes, stirring halfway through and adding the sugar. The tomatoes will be roasted and softened.

Place in a jug with the Worcestershire sauce and tomato purée and blend with a stick blender, or in a food processor, until smooth, then season to taste. Allow to cool, then store in an airtight container in the refrigerator for up to a week.

Cook the bacon in a single layer in a preheated air fryer at 180°C (350°F) for 6–8 minutes, turning halfway through, until cooked to your liking.

Butter 2 slices of the bread, top each with 2 rashers of bacon and spoon over some ketchup. Top with the remaining bread and cut in half. Serve immediately.

For sausage & onion baps, cook 2 sausages in a preheated air fryer at 180°C (350°F) for 6 minutes, then turn and add 4 small onion wedges spritzed with a little sunflower oil. Cook for a further 7–8 minutes, or until the sausages are cooked through and the onions tender. To serve, split 2 white baps, cut each sausage in half lengthways, arrange on the baps and top with the onions and a dollop of brown sauce. Serve immediately.

soft-boiled eggs & soldiers

Serves **2**
Preparation time **2 minutes**
Cooking time **8 minutes**

2 **eggs**
2 slices of **bread**
butter, for spreading
salt and **pepper**

Place and cook the eggs in their shells in a preheated air fryer at 180°C (350°F) for 6 minutes. Remove and place in egg cups.

Cook the bread in the air fryer for 1 minute, then turn over and cook the other side for a further minute, until lightly toasted. Spread with the butter and cut into fingers.

Cut the tops off the eggs, season to taste and serve with the toast soldiers for dipping.

For easy fried eggs, place 1 teaspoon of sunflower oil in a cake tin and place in a preheated air fryer at 180°C (350°F) for 2 minutes. Crack 1 egg into a small dish, then add to the hot oil. Repeat with a second egg. Cook for 3–4 minutes, until the white is set but the yolk is still runny. Serve on toast with a good grind of black pepper and a little salt.

potato rösti with smoked salmon

Serves **4**
Preparation time **12 minutes**
Cooking time **26 minutes**

2 **floury potatoes**, about 450 g
  (14½ oz), scrubbed
1 tablespoon chopped **chives**
1 teaspoon **olive oil**, plus extra
  for spritzing
150 g (5 oz) **reduced-fat
  crème fraîche**
4 tablespoons chopped **dill**
1 tablespoon **capers**, rinsed
  and finely chopped
finely grated zest of ½ **lemon**
200 g (7 oz) **smoked salmon
  slices**
salt and **pepper**

Cook the potatoes in a saucepan of lightly salted boiling water for 8 minutes, then drain. When cool enough to handle, coarsely grate the potatoes into a bowl, add the chives and season with salt and pepper. Stir to mix.

Place the oil in an 18 cm (7 inch) round cake tin and place in a preheated air fryer at 180°C (350°F) for 3 minutes.

Press the potato mixture in an even layer into the tin, then spritz the top with oil and cook for 12–15 minutes, until the rösti is crispy and tender.

Meanwhile, mix the crème fraîche with the dill, capers and lemon zest and season to taste. Tip the rösti on to a board and cut into 4 wedges. Serve the wedges topped with the crème fraîche and slices of smoked salmon.

For ham & cheese rösti, parboil and grate the potatoes as above, then stir in 4 chopped spring onions, 150 g (5 oz) of grated Cheddar or Gruyère cheese and 125 g (4 oz) of chopped ham. Cook as above and serve in wedges with a poached egg on top of each.

iced cinnamon rolls

Makes **12**
Preparation time **10 minutes**
Cooking time **16 minutes**

1 tablespoon **ground cinnamon**
3 tablespoons **caster sugar**
1 sheet of **ready-rolled puff pastry**
1 **egg**, beaten

Icing
50 g (2 oz) **icing sugar**
1–2 teaspoons **cold water**

Mix the cinnamon and caster sugar in a bowl. Unroll the pastry sheet and sprinkle all over with the sugar, leaving a 1 cm (½ inch) border on one of the shorter edges. Spread out the sugar evenly with the back of a spoon.

Brush a little of the beaten egg on the uncovered border, then roll the pastry from the opposite edge. Press to seal.

Cut into 12 equal slices, each about 2 cm (¾ inch) thick. Arrange the slices in a 20 cm (8 inch) round cake tin so just touching, and brush with the remaining egg. Cook in a preheated air fryer at 190°C (375°F) for 15–16 minutes, until golden, risen and the base is crispy.

Meanwhile, mix the icing sugar with 1 teaspoon of the measured water, adding a little more water if necessary, until the icing is thick and just runs off the spoon.

Transfer the rolls to a wire rack and drizzle over the icing. Serve warm.

For apricot & pistachio palmiers, unroll the sheet of puff pastry, spread with 6 tablespoons of apricot jam and scatter over 100 g (3½ oz) of chopped pistachios. Roll in both of the long sides until they meet in the centre. Use a sharp knife to cut into 2 cm (¾ inch) thick slices, so you have 12 palmiers. Mix together 2 teaspoons of caster sugar and ½ teaspoon of ground cinnamon. Brush a little milk over the pastries, then roll the sides in the cinnamon sugar. Cook in batches, cut sides up, in a preheated air fryer, sprinkled with the remaining sugar, at 190°C (375°F) for 12–15 minutes until golden, risen and crisp.

apricot & cinnamon cereal bars

Makes **8**
Preparation time **10 minutes**
Cooking time **16 minutes**

75 g (3 oz) **butter**, plus extra for
   greasing
2 tablespoons **honey**
75 g (3 oz) **light soft brown
   sugar**
1 teaspoon **ground cinnamon**
125 g (4 oz) **porridge oats**
25 g (1 oz) **cornflakes**
25 g (1 oz) **mixed seeds**, such
   as sunflower, pumpkin and
   sesame
50 g (2 oz) **soft dried apricots**,
   chopped
25 g (1 oz) **raisins**

Grease a 15 cm (6 inch) square cake tin. In a large
saucepan, gently melt the honey, butter, sugar and
cinnamon over a low heat, stirring, until the sugar
has dissolved.

Remove from the heat and gently stir in all the
remaining ingredients, until well combined. Tip into
the prepared tin and gently press down with the back
of a spoon to even the top. Cover the tin with foil.

Cook in a preheated air fryer at 180°C (350°F)
for 10 minutes, then uncover and cook for a further
4 minutes, until golden on top. Leave to cool in the
tin, then cut into 8 bars.

For berry & ginger bars, prepare and cook as above,
substituting the cinnamon with 1 teaspoon of ground
ginger and the apricots and raisins with 75 g (3 oz)
of dried mixed berries, such as cranberries, cherries,
blueberries and strawberries.

marmalade & seed muffins

Makes **4**
Preparation time **10 minutes**
Cooking time **15 minutes**

6 tablespoons **thick-cut orange marmalade**
3 tablespoons **sunflower** or **light olive oil**
1 **egg**
3 tablespoons **milk**
125 g (4 oz) **plain flour**
1 teaspoon **baking powder**
½ teaspoon **ground cinnamon**
½ teaspoon **salt**
2 tablespoons **mixed seeds**, such as sunflower, pumpkin and linseed
1 tablespoon **caster sugar**

Line 4 small ramekins or cake tins with paper muffin cases. In a jug, whisk 4 tablespoons of the marmalade with the oil, egg and milk.

Stir together the flour, baking powder, cinnamon, salt, seeds and sugar in a large bowl and stir the wet ingredients into the dry ingredients until just combined.

Divide the mixture equally between the cases. Cook the muffins in a preheated air fryer at 160°C (325°F) for 14–15 minutes, or until a cocktail stick inserted into a muffin comes out clean.

Allow to cool slightly on a wire rack, then warm the remaining marmalade and spoon over the muffins. Serve warm or cold.

For banana & oat muffins, mash 1 ripe banana with the sunflower oil and beaten egg. Place 100 g (3½ oz) of plain flour and 25 g (1 oz) of porridge oats in a bowl with the baking powder, cinnamon, salt, mixed seeds and sugar and stir well. Stir the banana mixture into the dry ingredients, then place in the muffin cases as above. Top each muffin with a slice of dried banana and cook as above.

quick snacks

courgette & sweetcorn fritters

Makes **8**
Preparation time **10 minutes**
Cooking time **10 minutes**

1 large **courgette**, coarsely
   grated
75 g (3 oz) drained canned
   sweetcorn
1 **red chilli**, deseeded and
   finely chopped
2 tablespoons chopped **mint**
50 g (2 oz) **self-raising flour**
1 **egg**, lightly beaten
50 g (2 oz) **ricotta cheese**
olive oil, for spritzing
salt and **pepper**

To serve
sweet chilli sauce
crisp **green salad**

Squeeze the grated courgette in a clean tea towel to
remove excess water, then place in a large bowl. Add
the sweetcorn, chilli, mint and flour, then stir in the egg.
Mix well and season with salt and pepper. Gently fold
in the ricotta.

Place heaped tablespoons of the batter on a piece of
pierced nonstick baking paper in a preheated air fryer,
flatten slightly with the back of a spoon and spritz with
oil. Cook at 190°C (375°F) for 6 minutes. Flip over and
cook for a further 3–4 minutes, until golden. You may
need to do this in 2 batches to make 8 in total.

Serve 2 fritters per person, drizzled with a little sweet
chilli sauce, with a crisp green salad on the side.

For feta, pea & courgette fritters, make the fritters
as above, substituting the ricotta with 125 g (4 oz) of
crumbled feta. Defrost 75 g (3 oz) of frozen peas and
use instead of the sweetcorn. Cook as above and serve
with tomato salsa.

crispy salt & pepper chickpeas

Serves **4**

Preparation time **5 minutes,**
   plus cooling

Cooking time **20 minutes**

400 g (13 oz) can **chickpeas,**
   drained and rinsed

2 teaspoons **olive oil**

1 teaspoon **sea salt**

1 teaspoon freshly ground
   black pepper

Dry the chickpeas on kitchen paper to remove any excess water, then remove any loose skins.

Mix together the oil, salt and pepper in a bowl, add the chickpeas and toss in the mixture to ensure they are evenly coated.

Cook in a preheated air fryer at 200°C (400°F) for 15–20 minutes, shaking the basket occasionally, until crispy. Allow to cool as they will continue to crisp. Serve as a snack or as a salad topper.

For sriracha & honey-roasted chickpeas, prepare the chickpeas as above and place in a bowl. Stir in 1 tablespoon of sriracha sauce, 1 tablespoon of honey, 2 teaspoons of sesame seeds, ½ teaspoon of salt and a pinch of pepper. Cook as above until golden and crispy.

spiced tortilla chips

Serves **4**
Preparation time **15 minutes**
Cooking time **16 minutes**

6 **mini corn** or **flour tortillas**
2 teaspoons **sunflower oil**
1 tablespoon **Mexican spice mix**
salt and **pepper**

Dipping sauce
1 large **mango**, peeled and pitted
1 tablespoon **olive oil**
finely grated zest and juice of ½ **lime**
1 **red jalapeño chilli**, deseeded and finely chopped
2 tablespoons finely chopped **fresh coriander**

To serve
ready-made **guacamole**
salsa (see right)

Brush both sides of the tortillas with a little oil, then sprinkle over the spice mix and season with a little salt and pepper.

Stack the tortillas on top of each other and cut into 6, so you have 36 tortilla chips.

Separate out the tortillas and cook half in a preheated air fryer at 160°C (325°F) for 6 minutes, shaking halfway through. Remove any chips that are golden, then cook the remainder for a further 1–2 minutes until golden. Transfer to a wire rack – they will continue to crisp as they cool. Cook the remaining tortillas in the same way.

Meanwhile, finely chop one-third of the mango and set aside. Roughly chop the rest and place in a small food processor with the oil, lime zest and juice and chilli and blitz until smooth, or use a stick blender. Transfer to a bowl and stir in the reserved mango and fresh coriander. Season to taste and serve the tortillas with the dipping sauce, ready-made guacamole and salsa (see below).

For tomato salsa dip, to serve as an accompaniment, finely chop 3 spring onions and place them in a bowl with the juice of ½ lime. Add 500 g (1 lb) of tomatoes, chopped into rough dice, 1 deseeded and finely chopped green jalapeño chilli and 2 tablespoons of chopped fresh coriander. Season to taste with salt and leave to sit for 30 minutes before serving.

sesame prawn toasts

Makes **16**
Preparation time **10 minutes**
Cooking time **16 minutes**

250 g (8 oz) **raw peeled prawns**, deveined and roughly chopped
1 teaspoon grated **fresh root ginger**
½ teaspoon **salt**
3 **spring onions**, finely chopped
1 tablespoon **cornflour**
1 teaspoon **toasted sesame oil**
1 **egg white**
4 slices of slightly stale **white bread**, crusts removed
2 tablespoons **sesame seeds**
sunflower oil, for spritzing
sweet chilli sauce or **sweet and sour dipping sauce**

Place the prawns in a food processor with the ginger, salt, 2 of the spring onions, cornflour, sesame oil and egg white. Blitz to a paste.

Spread the mixture thickly on to the slices of bread, then sprinkle with the sesame seeds. Cut each slice of bread into quarters to make 16 triangles.

Place half the toasts in a single layer, prawn sides up, in a preheated air fryer. Spritz with a little oil and cook at 200°C (400°F) for 8 minutes, until golden and crispy. Repeat with the remaining toasts. Serve hot with sweet chilli sauce or sweet and sour dipping sauce, garnished with the remaining spring onion.

For prawn spring rolls, mix 50 g (2 oz) of bean sprouts in a bowl with ½ carrot, cut into matchsticks, 3 thinly sliced spring onions and ¼ red pepper, deseeded and cut into thin strips. Add 125 g (4 oz) of chopped raw peeled prawns, 1 crushed garlic clove, 2 teaspoons of grated fresh root ginger and 2 teaspoons of dark soy sauce and mix well. Stack 4 sheets of filo pastry together and cut in half. Place 1 piece of the pastry on a board and brush the edges with a little oil. Place one-eighth of the filling on the bottom edge. Roll up, folding the sides in as you go. Repeat with the remaining pastry and filling to make 8 spring rolls. Brush with oil and cook in batches in a preheated air fryer at 180°C (350°F) for 8–10 minutes, turning halfway through, until golden. Serve with soy sauce.

parmesan kale crisps

Serves **3–4**

Preparation time **10 minutes**

Cooking time **10 minutes**

200 g (7 oz) **kale**

2 teaspoons **olive oil**

25 g (1 oz) **Parmesan cheese**, grated

½ teaspoon **salt**

Cut the kale leaves away from the spines, then cut into 3.5 cm (1½ inch) pieces. Place in a large bowl and drizzle over the oil. Use your hands to make sure the leaves are coated, then sprinkle over the cheese and salt and toss to coat.

Cook in batches in a single layer in a preheated air fryer at 190°C (375°F) for 3–5 minutes, checking them after 3 minutes and transferring any that are crisp to a wire rack. These are best eaten the day they are made.

For spiced kale crisps, prepare the kale as above, add the oil, then omit the cheese and sprinkle over 2 teaspoons of ras el hanout seasoning, 2 teaspoons of finely grated lime zest and the salt, and cook as above.

spicy crabcakes with lime-chilli dip

Makes **12**

Preparation time **10 minutes, plus chilling**

Cooking time **10 minutes**

150 g (5 oz) **skinless, boneless cod** or **haddock**, roughly chopped

100 g (3½ oz) **mixed white and brown crab meat**

2 teaspoons grated **fresh root ginger**

1 **Thai red chilli**, deseeded and chopped

2 teaspoons **Thai fish sauce**

2 teaspoons **palm** or **light soft brown sugar**

1 tablespoon **lime juice**

2 tablespoons chopped **fresh coriander**, plus extra to garnish

1 **egg white**

3 tablespoons **cornflour**

2 **spring onions**, thinly sliced

2 teaspoons **sunflower oil**

Lime chilli dipping sauce

2 tablespoons **rice wine vinegar**

1 **Thai red chilli**, deseeded and finely chopped

grated zest and juice of **1 lime**

2 teaspoons **caster sugar**

Place all the ingredients for the crabcakes, except the spring onions and oil, in a food processor and blend to a smooth paste. Stir in the spring onions, then with damp hands, shape the mixture into 12 small patties. Chill for at least 15 minutes in the refrigerator.

Whisk together all the ingredients for the dipping sauce until the sugar has dissolved.

Brush the crabcakes with a little oil and place in a single layer on a piece of pierced nonstick baking paper in a preheated air fryer. Cook at 190°C (375°F) for 4–6 minutes. Turn over, brush with a little more oil and cook for a further 4 minutes, until golden brown and cooked through. You may need to do this in 2 batches. Garnish with coriander leaves and serve immediately with the dipping sauce.

For lemon & herb crabcakes, cook 200 g (7 oz) of chopped potatoes in a saucepan of lightly salted water for 10–12 minutes, until tender. Drain well and mash. Place in a bowl and stir in 150 g (5 oz) of mixed crab meat, ½ teaspoon of Dijon mustard, the finely grated zest of 1 lemon and 2 tablespoons of chopped basil. Season well and shape into 8 small cakes. Place 1 beaten egg in a bowl and 75 g (3 oz) of fine dried breadcrumbs on a plate. Dip each crabcake in the beaten egg, then coat in the crumbs. Place in batches in a preheated air fryer, spritz with oil and cook at 190°C (375°F) for 8–10 minutes, turning halfway through and spritzing with a little more oil. Serve with mayonnaise for dipping.

vegetable samosas

Makes **16**
Preparation time **20 minutes,
  plus resting**
Cooking time **24 minutes**

75 g (3 oz) **potato**, peeled and
  cut into 1 cm (½ inch) dice
1 **onion**, cut into 1 cm (½ inch)
  dice
1 small **carrot**, cut into 1 cm
  (½ inch) dice
2 teaspoons **sunflower oil**
1 teaspoon **cumin seeds**
50 g (2 oz) **frozen peas**,
  defrosted
1 tablespoon **medium curry
  paste**
2 tablespoons chopped **fresh
  coriander**, plus extra leaves
  to garnish
salt and **pepper**
mango chutney, to serve

Pastry
225 g (7½ oz) **plain flour**, plus
  extra for dusting
1 teaspoon **salt**
2 tablespoons **sunflower oil**,
  plus extra for spritzing
100 ml (3½ fl oz) **cold water**

Mix the flour and salt for the pastry in a bowl. Make
a well in the centre and add the oil. Mix the ingredients
by hand to form crumbs. Slowly add the water to make
a firm dough. Transfer to a lightly floured surface. Knead
for 5–10 minutes, until smooth. Roll into a ball, place in a
plastic bag and rest at room temperature for 30 minutes.

Place the potato, onion, carrot, oil, cumin seeds, salt and
pepper in an ovenproof dish. Place in a preheated air
fryer and cook at 180°C (350°F) for 10 minutes, until
just tender. Transfer to a bowl, stir in the peas, curry
paste and fresh coriander and gently mix. Leave to cool.

Divide the dough into 8 equal pieces, then roll one out to
a 15 cm (6 inch) disc. Cut in half to make 2 semi-circles.
Brush the straight edge of one with a little water, then fold
one corner to the centre of the curved edge and bring the
other corner up over the top to make a cone. Fill with a
tablespoon of the filling. Seal the open edges together with
a little water. Repeat with the remaining filling and dough.

Place half the samosas in a single layer in a preheated
air fryer, spritz with oil and cook at 180°C (350°F) for
10–12 minutes, turning halfway through, until golden.
Repeat with the remaining samosas. Garnish with
coriander leaves and serve with mango chutney.

For sweet potato & spinach samosas, prepare the
filling as above, substituting the potato with sweet potato.
Place 125 g (4 oz) of spinach in a colander and pour over
boiling water, until it wilts. Cool, then roughly chop. Stir the
spinach into the potato mixture, with the curry paste and
coriander. Prepare and cook the samosas as above.

spiced prawn popcorn

Serves **4**
Preparation time **15 minutes**
Cooking time **8 minutes**

1 **egg white**
2 tablespoons **buttermilk**
1 tablespoon **Cajun spice mix**
finely grated zest of 1 **lime**
300 g (10 oz) **raw peeled**
  king prawns, deveined
75 g (3 oz) **plain flour**
sunflower oil, for spritzing
salt and **pepper**

Zingy lime dip
50 ml (2 fl oz) **light**
  mayonnaise
50 ml (2 fl oz) **soured cream**
finely grated zest of 1 **lime**
2 tablespoons **lime juice**
1 tablespoons chopped **fresh**
  coriander

Place all the ingredients for the dip in a bowl and mix together, then season to taste.

Whisk the egg white in a bowl until frothy, then stir in the buttermilk, spice mix and lime zest. Add the prawns and turn to coat in the mixture.

Place the flour on a plate and season with salt and pepper, add the prawns and toss to coat in the flour.

Arrange half the prawns in a single layer in a preheated air fryer and spritz with oil. Cook at 200°C (400°F) for 4 minutes, turning once, until cooked through and crispy. Repeat with the remaining prawns, then serve with the lime dip.

For coconut prawns, place 75 g (3 oz) of desiccated coconut in a food processor with 25 g (1 oz) of dried breadcrumbs and pulse until the coconut has broken down. Transfer to a bowl. Place 4 tablespoons of cornflour on a plate and season with salt and pepper. Place the egg white in a bowl and beat until frothy. Toss the prawns, a few at a time, in the cornflour and shake off the excess, then dip in the egg white to coat completely. Shake off any excess, then coat in the coconut mixture. Spritz with a little oil and cook in the air fryer as above.

chilli & paprika vegetable crisps

Serves **4**

Preparation time **10 minutes**

Cooking time **28 minutes**

1 small **sweet potato**, scrubbed

1 **beetroot**, scrubbed

1 **parsnip**, scrubbed

2 teaspoons **chilli-flavoured oil**

2 teaspoons **smoked paprika**, plus extra for sprinkling

1 teaspoon **sea salt**

Slice the vegetables thinly, using a mandolin or a sharp knife, to about 2.5 mm (⅛ inch) thick. Place in a large bowl, add the oil and turn to coat the vegetables, then add the paprika and salt and toss to coat.

Cook half the vegetable slices in a single layer in a preheated air fryer at 150°C (300°F) for 12 minutes, turning halfway through. Remove any crisps that are golden, then cook the remainder for a further 1–2 minutes, until golden. Transfer to a wire rack – they will continue to crisp as they cool. Repeat with the remaining vegetable slices.

Sprinkle the vegetable crisps with a little extra paprika before serving.

For garlic & herb vegetable crisps, prepare the vegetables as above, then toss in 2 teaspoons of garlic oil, 2 teaspoons of dried mixed herbs, salt and pepper. Cook as above.

light bites

frittata with nduja & ricotta

Serves **4**
Preparation time **5 minutes**
Cooking time **12 minutes**

olive oil, for greasing
4 **eggs**
125 g (4 oz) **ricotta cheese**
6 **Sweet Drop** or **piquant
    peppers** from a jar, drained
    and chopped
4 tablespoons chopped **basil**
15 g (½ oz) **nduja**
salt and **pepper**
rocket leaves, to serve

Grease the base and sides of an 18 cm (7 inch) nonstick round cake tin. Beat the eggs in a small bowl with the ricotta and season with salt and pepper.

Stir in the peppers and basil, then pour into the prepared tin. Dot with the nduja. Cook in a preheated air fryer at 160°C (325°F) for 12 minutes, until set and golden.

Allow to cool in the tin for a few minutes, then remove and cut into 4 slices. Serve with rocket leaves.

For ham, pea & mint frittata, place 200 g (7 oz) of frozen peas in a bowl, cover with boiling water and allow to stand for 2–3 minutes, then drain well. Meanwhile, beat the eggs with the ricotta and 2 tablespoons of chopped mint. Season and stir in 100 g (3½ oz) of shredded ham hock and the peas. Pour into the prepared tin and cook as above.

chicken wings & blue cheese dip

Serves **4**
Preparation time **10 minutes**
Cooking time **15 minutes**

500 g (1 lb) **chicken wings**
2 teaspoons **olive oil**
2 teaspoons **smoked paprika**
1 teaspoon **garlic powder**
1 teaspoon **onion powder**
salt and **pepper**

Blue cheese dip
50 g (2 oz) **soft blue cheese**, such as Gorgonzola or dolcelatte
75 ml (3 fl oz) **soured cream**
1 teaspoon **lemon juice**
1 tablespoon chopped **chives**

Place the chicken wings in a bowl, add the olive oil, smoked paprika, garlic powder and onion powder and toss well, so the chicken wings are evenly coated.

Cook in a single layer in a preheated air fryer at 200°C (400°F) for 10 minutes, then turn over and cook for a further 5 minutes, until the skin is crispy and the chicken is cooked through.

Meanwhile, mash together all the ingredients for the dip until well combined. Serve the wings with the dip.

For gochujang chicken wings, place the wings in a bowl with the olive oil and season with salt and pepper. Cook as above for 10 minutes. Meanwhile, place 2 tablespoons of rice wine vinegar in a saucepan with 1 tablespoon each of soft brown sugar and dark soy sauce, 1 crushed garlic clove, 1 teaspoon of grated fresh root ginger and 1 tablespoon of gochujang (Korean red pepper paste). Cook over a medium heat, stirring, until all the ingredients are combined, then simmer for 3 minutes, until glossy and slightly thickened. Brush the wings all over with the glaze and cook for a further 5 minutes, until sticky and cooked through.

reuben toasted sandwich

Serves **1–2**
Preparation time **4 minutes**
Cooking time **8 minutes**

1 tablespoon **mayonnaise**
1 teaspoon **French mustard**
2 slices of **light rye bread**
4 slices of **salt beef**
1 slice of **Gruyère cheese**
2 tablespoons **sauerkraut**, drained
1 **gherkin**, sliced lengthways
1 tablespoon melted **butter**

Mix the mayonnaise and mustard together, then spread over 1 slice of the bread. Top with the salt beef, cheese, sauerkraut and sliced gherkin. Place the other slice of bread on top and spread the top of the sandwich with half the butter.

Place the sandwich, butter side down, in a preheated air fryer, then brush the remaining butter over the top. Cook at 190°C (375°F) for 4 minutes, then carefully flip over and cook for a further 3–4 minutes, until the cheese has melted and the bread is toasted. Cut in half and serve immediately.

For kimchi & cheese sourdough toastie, place a slice of sourdough on a board and top with a slice of mature Cheddar cheese, a slice of mozzarella and 50 g (2 oz) of drained kimchi. Top with a second slice of sourdough, then butter the bread and cook the sandwich as above, until the cheese has melted. Cut in half and serve immediately.

roasted cauliflower tabbouleh

Serves **4**

Preparation time **15 minutes, plus cooling**

Cooking time **12 minutes**

½ **cauliflower**, cut into 2.5 cm (1 inch) florets

2 teaspoons **olive oil**

1 teaspoon **Baharat** or **Middle Eastern spice mix**

100 g (3½ oz) **bulgur wheat**

300 g (10 oz) **tomatoes**, finely chopped

¼ **cucumber**, deseeded and diced

5 **spring onions**, thinly sliced

150 g (5 oz) **pomegranate seeds**

6 tablespoons chopped **flat leaf parsley**

4 tablespoons chopped **mint**

Dressing

2 tablespoons **olive oil**

juice of **1 lemon**

salt and **pepper**

Place the cauliflower florets in a bowl, drizzle over the oil, sprinkle over the spice mix and toss well to coat. Cook in a preheated air fryer at 180°C (350°F) for 12 minutes, shaking the basket a couple of times, until crisp.

Meanwhile, place the bulgur wheat in a saucepan of lightly salted cold water, bring to the boil and simmer for 8–10 minutes, until tender. Drain well, then spread out on a baking sheet to cool.

Place the cooled bulgur wheat and cauliflower in a bowl, then gently stir in the tomatoes, cucumber, spring onions, pomegranate seeds and herbs.

Whisk together the dressing ingredients, pour over the tabbouleh, mix well and serve immediately.

For harissa-roasted cauliflower with couscous,

place the cauliflower florets in a bowl with 1 tablespoon of harissa paste, 1 teaspoon of olive oil and 1 teaspoon of ground cumin and cook as above. Place 200 g (7 oz) of couscous in a large bowl and pour over 300 ml (½ pint) of hot vegetable stock. Leave for 5 minutes until all the liquid has been absorbed, then fluff up with a fork and allow to cool slightly. Toss the cauliflower into the couscous with the spring onions, pomegranate seeds and chopped mint, omitting the tomatoes, cucumber and parsley, then scatter over 200 g (7 oz) of crumbled feta cheese. Make a tahini dressing by mixing 100 ml (3½ fl oz) of tahini with the juice of ½ lemon and 3 tablespoons of warm water. Drizzle over the salad and serve.

falafel bowls

Serves **4**

Preparation time **20 minutes, plus chilling**

Cooking time **10 minutes**

400 g (13 oz) can **chickpeas**, drained and rinsed

1 **garlic clove**, crushed

1 teaspoon **ground cumin**

½ teaspoon **ground coriander**

2 tablespoons chopped **flat leaf parsley**

½ teaspoon **salt**

1 teaspoon **baking powder**

1 tablespoon **plain flour**

1 tablespoon **lemon juice**

2 teaspoons **olive oil**, plus extra for spritzing

pepper

Tahini dressing

4 tablespoons **tahini**

juice of ½ **lemon**

4 tablespoons **cold water**

To serve

250 g (8 oz) cooked **quinoa**

2 **carrots**, grated

4 **tomatoes**, quartered

½ **cucumber**, deseeded and chopped

Place the chickpeas, garlic, spices, parsley and salt in a food processor, season with pepper and pulse until coarsely chopped. Add the baking powder, flour, lemon juice and oil and pulse until well combined.

Divide the mixture into 12 and roll into balls, then flatten slightly. Cover and chill in the refrigerator for 30 minutes.

Place in a preheated air fryer, spritz with a little oil and cook at 180°C (350°F) for 10 minutes, turning halfway through.

Meanwhile, mix together the dressing ingredients and season to taste. Divide the quinoa, carrots, tomatoes and cucumber between 4 bowls. Top each bowl with 3 falafel and drizzle over the tahini dressing.

For spicy pea & mint falafel, place 250 g (8 oz) of frozen peas in a bowl, cover with boiling water, leave to stand for 2–3 minutes, then drain well. Place the chickpeas, peas, 4 tablespoons of chopped mint, 2 teaspoons of harissa paste, the baking powder, flour, salt and pepper in a food processor and pulse until combined. Divide the mixture into 16, roll into balls and flatten slightly. Cook as above and serve with flatbreads, salad and the tahini dressing.

jalapeño poppers

Makes **14**
Preparation time **10 minutes**
Cooking time **8 minutes**

7 **jalapeño chillies**
125 g (4 oz) **cream cheese**
50 g (2 oz) **mozzarella**, grated
4 crispy cooked **streaky bacon rashers**, chopped into small pieces
2 **spring onions**, finely chopped
2 tablespoons **panko breadcrumbs**
½ teaspoon **smoked paprika**
olive oil, for spritzing
salt and **pepper**
ready-made **soured cream and chive dip**, to serve

Cut each jalapeño in half lengthways and use a small spoon to remove the membrane and seeds and discard them. In a bowl, mix together the cream cheese, mozzarella, bacon pieces and spring onions and season to taste. Spoon the cream cheese mixture into the jalapeño halves.

Mix the breadcrumbs with the paprika, then dip the cream cheese side of each jalapeño in the breadcrumb mixture.

Place the stuffed jalapeños, breadcrumb sides up, in a preheated air fryer, spritz with a little oil and cook at 190°C (375°F) for 7–8 minutes, until the cheese has melted, the chilli has softened and the topping is crispy. Serve immediately with a ready-made soured cream and chive dip.

For chorizo & goats' cheese poppers, place 75 g (3 oz) of diced chorizo in a dry frying pan and cook for 2–3 minutes, until starting to crisp. Drain on kitchen paper to remove the excess oil. Prepare the chillies as above. Place 125 g (4 oz) of soft goats' cheese in a bowl, stir in the chorizo, 50 g (2 oz) of grated Cheddar cheese and the spring onions. Season well and use the mixture to fill the chillies. Dip in the breadcrumb mixture and cook as above.

halloumi with spicy dipping sauce

Serves **4–6**
Preparation time **10 minutes**
Cooking time **12 minutes**

2 x 225 g (7½ oz) pack
  halloumi cheese
4 tablespoons **plain flour**
½ teaspoon **dried oregano**
½ teaspoon **smoked paprika**
½ teaspoon **garlic powder**
sunflower oil, for spritzing
pepper

Spicy dipping sauce
150 ml (5 fl oz) **Greek yogurt**
finely grated zest of ½ **lemon**
1 tablespoon **harissa paste**

Cut the halloumi into sticks about 1.5 cm (¾ inch) thick. On a plate, mix together the flour, oregano, paprika and garlic powder and season with pepper. Add the halloumi sticks and turn to coat in the flour.

Place half the halloumi sticks in a single layer in a preheated air fryer, spritz with a little oil and cook at 180°C (350°F) for 6 minutes, turning halfway through, until golden and crispy. Repeat with the remaining halloumi sticks.

Meanwhile, mix the yogurt for the dipping sauce with the lemon zest and swirl through the harissa paste. Serve the halloumi sticks immediately with the dip.

For pesto bocconcini balls, place 2 tablespoons of plain flour on a plate and season with salt and pepper. Place 1 tablespoon of sundried tomato pesto in a bowl and beat 1 egg in another bowl. Roll 20 mozzarella balls first in the flour, then in the pesto, then dip in the egg and finally coat in 50 g (2 oz) of fine dried breadcrumbs. Repeat with the egg and breadcrumbs to double coat, then chill for 10 minutes. Spritz the balls with oil and cook in a preheated air fryer at 180°C (350°F) for 4–5 minutes, until just crispy and the cheese is starting to melt. Serve immediately.

pancetta crustless quiche

Serves **4**
Preparation time **5 minutes**
Cooking time **30 minutes**

butter, for greasing
8 thin slices of **pancetta**
4 **eggs**
150 ml (¼ pint) **double cream**
50 g (2 oz) **Parmesan
cheese**, grated
50 g (2 oz) **soft blue cheese**,
cut into small pieces
12 **cherry tomatoes**, halved
pepper
**watercress, spinach and
rocket salad**, to serve

Grease a 20 cm (8 inch) quiche tin or ovenproof dish.
Cook the pancetta in a single layer in a preheated air
fryer at 180°C (350°F) for 4–5 minutes, until crispy.
Drain on kitchen paper and cut into pieces.

Whisk the eggs and cream together in a bowl, stir
in the cheeses and season with pepper. Stir in half
the tomatoes and pancetta. Pour into the prepared
tin and add the remaining tomatoes and pancetta.

Place the tin in a preheated air fryer and cook at 160°C
(325°F) for 24–26 minutes, covering the top with foil if
it becomes too brown, until set.

Allow to cool in the tin slightly before cutting into slices.
Serve with a watercress, spinach and rocket salad.

For salmon & courgette crustless quiche, trim the
ends off 1 courgette and use a vegetable peeler to slice
it into ribbons. Whisk together the eggs and cream, then
stir in the Parmesan with 50 g (2 oz) of grated Cheddar
and 200 g (7 oz) of drained and flaked canned salmon.
Arrange half the courgette ribbons in the bottom of the
prepared tin, then pour over the egg mixture and add the
remaining courgette ribbons. Cook as above.

miso mushrooms on sourdough

Serves **2**

Preparation time **5 minutes**

Cooking time **8 minutes**

2 teaspoons **white** or **brown miso paste**

1 teaspoon **dark soy sauce**

1 **garlic clove**, crushed

2 teaspoons **olive oil**

200 g (7 oz) **mushrooms**, such as chestnut or Portobello, roughly chopped

4 tablespoons **vegan cream**

2 slices of **sourdough bread**, toasted

pepper

2 tablespoons chopped **flat leaf parsley**, to garnish

Mix the miso paste, soy sauce, garlic and oil in a bowl and season well with pepper. Add the mushrooms and turn to coat, then transfer to an ovenproof dish. Place the dish in a preheated air fryer and cook at 180°C (350°F) for 7 minutes, stirring once. Stir in the cream, then return to the air fryer and cook for 1 minute to heat through.

Spoon the mushrooms over the toast and sprinkle over the parsley. Serve immediately.

For creamy garlic & tarragon mushrooms, place the mushrooms in an ovenproof dish, drizzle over 2 teaspoons of garlic-flavoured oil and the crushed garlic clove, season well, stir to coat, then cook as above for 7 minutes. Stir in 2 teaspoons of lemon juice, the vegan cream and 1 tablespoon of chopped tarragon, return to the air fryer and cook for 1 minute more. Serve in bowls with warm crusty bread for dipping.

hot tortilla pizza

Serves **1**
Preparation time **3 minutes**
Cooking time **7 minutes**

1 **flour tortilla**, about 20 cm
   (8 inches) in diameter
olive oil, for spritzing
4 tablespoons **ready-made**
   pizza sauce
50 g (2 oz) **mozzarella**
   cheese, grated
4–5 slices of **pepperoni**
8 slices of fresh **red pepper**
6 **green jalapeño slices** from
   a jar
1 teaspoon **dried mixed herbs**

Spritz one side of the tortilla with a little oil and place, oil side down, in a preheated air fryer. Cook at 180°C (350°F) for 2 minutes, until starting to crisp.

Turn over the tortilla and spoon over the pizza sauce. Sprinkle with half the cheese, then top with the pepperoni, red pepper slices and jalapeños. Sprinkle over the remaining cheese and the dried mixed herbs and cook for a further 4–5 minutes, until the tortilla is crispy and the topping melted. Serve immediately with salad leaves, if you like.

For pizza Florentine, cook the tortilla on its own for 2 minutes as above. Meanwhile, place 50 g (2 oz) of baby spinach leaves in a colander and pour over boiling water to wilt. Allow to drain and when cool enough to handle, squeeze out the excess water. Turn the tortilla and spread with the pizza sauce, then top with the spinach and 50 g (2 oz) of grated mozzarella and crack an egg in the centre. Sprinkle over 15 g (½ oz) of grated Parmesan and a few chilli flakes. Cook as above until the egg is just set, but the yolk is still runny. Serve immediately.

goats' cheese toasts with walnuts

Serves **4**
Preparation time **2 minutes**
Cooking time **5 minutes**

4 small slices of **walnut bread**
1 **garlic clove**, peeled
2 x 200 g (7 oz) rounds of **soft goats' cheese with rind**
2 teaspoons chopped **thyme leaves**
4 **walnut halves**, roughly chopped
4 teaspoons **honey**
pepper

To serve
watercress
cherry tomatoes, halved

Cook the walnut bread in a preheated air fryer at 180°C (350°F) for 2 minutes, turning halfway through, until lightly toasted. You may need to do this in 2 batches. Rub the toast all over with the garlic clove.

Cut the round of goats' cheese into 4 slices, each about 1.5 cm (¾ inch) thick. Place each slice in the centre of a piece of toast and sprinkle with the thyme leaves, walnuts and pepper. Return to the air fryer and cook for 2–3 minutes, until the cheese starts to melt.

Drizzle with the honey and serve immediately with watercress and halved cherry tomatoes.

For caramelized onion & goats' cheese toasts, cut 4 slices of baguette on the diagonal and lightly toast in the air fryer as above. Spread each with 2 tablespoons of caramelized onion chutney, then top with the goats' cheese and some thyme leaves. Cook as above until the cheese has melted.

cheeseburger wraps

Serves **2**

Preparation time **10 minutes**

Cooking time **14 minutes**

2 **beef burgers**, about 100 g
(3½ oz) each

2 large **flour tortillas**

2 slices of **burger cheese**, or
other melting cheese such as
Jarlsberg

4 crispy cooked **streaky bacon
rashers**

2 tablespoons **barbecue** or
burger sauce, plus extra
to serve

2 **red onion** rings

handful of shredded **lettuce**

2 large slices of **tomato**

sunflower oil, for spritzing

Cook the burgers in a preheated air fryer at 180°C
(350°F) for 10 minutes, turning halfway through, until
cooked through.

Place 1 tortilla on a board and cut a slit from the bottom
edge to the middle of the tortilla. Imagine the tortilla
is divided into quarters. Place a cooked burger on the
bottom left quarter of the tortilla with a slice of cheese on
top. Place 2 rashers of crispy bacon on the top left quarter.
Spread half the sauce over the top right quarter and place
an onion ring on top, then arrange half the lettuce and
a slice of tomato on the bottom right quarter.

Fold the bottom left quarter of the tortilla over the top
left quarter and continue folding around the tortilla to
make a neat parcel. Repeat with the remaining tortilla and
ingredients. Spritz with a little oil and cook in a preheated
air fryer for 4 minutes, turning carefully halfway through,
until the tortilla is crispy and the cheese has melted. Cut
in half and serve immediately, with extra sauce.

For fish finger wraps, cook 4 frozen fish fingers in
a preheated air fryer at 200°C (400°F) for 6–7 minutes,
turning halfway through. Meanwhile, cut a slit in a tortilla
as above. Place 2 cooked fish fingers on the bottom
left quarter with a slice of cheese, then spread the next
quarter with 1 teaspoon of tartare sauce. Arrange a
small handful of rocket leaves on the top right quarter,
then spread 2 teaspoons of tomato ketchup on the last
quarter. Fold as above, then repeat with the remaining
tortilla and fish fingers. Spritz with a little oil and cook in
the air fryer for 2 minutes, until the cheese has melted.

vegetarian & vegan mains

mushroom burgers & kimchi slaw

Serves **4**
Preparation time **15 minutes**
Cooking time **12 minutes**

4 tablespoons **sesame seeds**
4 large **Portobello mushrooms**
crisp **green lettuce leaves**
4 **burger buns**, halved and toasted

Korean barbecue sauce
1 teaspoon **toasted sesame oil**
2 tablespoons **rice wine vinegar**
1 tablespoon **light soft brown sugar**
1 tablespoon **dark soy sauce**
1 **garlic clove**, crushed
1 teaspoon grated **fresh root ginger**
1 tablespoon **gochujang**

Kimchi slaw
4 tablespoons **vegan mayonnaise**
4 tablespoons **vegan kimchi**, roughly chopped
4 **spring onions**, chopped
1 small **carrot**, coarsely grated

Place all the sauce ingredients in a small saucepan over a medium heat and cook, stirring, until all the ingredients are combined, then simmer for 3 minutes, until glossy and slightly thickened. Set aside.

Combine all the slaw ingredients in a bowl and mix well.

Place the sesame seeds on a plate. Hold each mushroom by the stalk and brush it all over with the sauce, then dip in the seeds to lightly coat.

Arrange the mushrooms, gill sides down, in a preheated air fryer and cook at 200°C (400°F) for 5 minutes, then turn over and cook for a further 4 minutes, until tender.

Pile some lettuce leaves on the base of each bun and top with a mushroom and a generous amount of the slaw. Top with the lids and serve immediately.

For sesame-glazed aubergines, cut 1 large aubergine into 1.5 cm (¾ inch) thick slices and brush one side of each slice with oil and sprinkle with a little salt. Place in a preheated air fryer, oiled sides up, and cook at 180°C (350°F) for 8 minutes, turning halfway through and spritzing with a little more oil. Meanwhile, make the sauce as above. Reduce the temperature of the air fryer to 160°C (325°F) and toss the aubergine slices in the sauce so they are coated all over. Cook in the air fryer for 6–8 minutes, until tender, glazed and sticky. Serve on rice, sprinkled with chopped spring onions and 2 tablespoons of sesame seeds.

teriyaki tofu & vegetable kebabs

Serves **4**

Preparation time **15 minutes,
plus pressing and
marinating**

Cooking time **12 minutes**

400 g (13 oz) **firm tofu**

1 **red pepper**, cored,
deseeded and cut into cubes

4 **spring onions**, cut into
2.5 cm (1 inch) pieces

1 tablespoon toasted **sesame
seeds**

steamed **rice**, to serve

Marinade

2 tablespoons **dark soy sauce**

1 tablespoon **mirin** or **rice
wine vinegar**

1 tablespoon **light soft brown
sugar**

1 **garlic clove**, crushed

2 teaspoons finely grated
fresh root ginger

Place the tofu between 2 pieces of kitchen paper and place a chopping board or other heavy weight on top. Leave for at least 15 minutes to remove excess water, then cut into 24 cubes, about 2.5 cm (1 inch) across.

Mix all the marinade ingredients in a large bowl and stir until the sugar has dissolved. Stir in the tofu and leave to marinate for at least 1 hour, or overnight.

Thread the tofu pieces and vegetables alternately on to 8 small metal skewers, or 8 wooden skewers that have been soaked in water to prevent them burning.

Place in a single layer in a preheated air fryer and cook at 180°C (350°F) for 10–12 minutes, turning once and brushing generously all over with the remaining marinade halfway through.

Serve 2 kebabs per person, sprinkled with the toasted sesame seeds, with steamed rice.

For lemon tofu kebabs, prepare the tofu as above, but marinate in 2 tablespoons of olive oil, 1 crushed garlic clove, 2 tablespoons of lemon juice, 1 tablespoon of red wine vinegar and 2 teaspoons of dried mixed herbs. Thread on to skewers with 1 small red onion, cut into 8 wedges, 8 cherry tomatoes and 8 cubes of red or yellow pepper. Cook as above and serve with flatbreads and tzatziki, with a squeeze of lemon juice.

crispy nori tofu & chips

Serves **2**
Preparation time **10 minutes**
Cooking time **18 minutes**

200 g (7 oz) **firm tofu**, cut
    into 4 fingers about 2.5 cm
    (1 inch) thick
2 sheets of **nori**, halved
50 g (2 oz) **panko
    breadcrumbs**
250 g (8 oz) **frozen oven chips**
sunflower oil, for spritzing
salt and **pepper**

Batter
4 tablespoons **plain flour**
1 tablespoon **lemon juice**
3 tablespoons **cold water**

To serve
mushy peas
lemon wedges

Make the batter by placing the flour in a bowl and whisking in the lemon juice and measured water to make a thick consistency.

Season the tofu with salt and pepper and wrap each finger in a piece of nori, dampening the edges with a little water to seal – the moisture in the tofu will help it stick. Dip each finger in the batter to fully coat, then in the breadcrumbs.

Cook the chips in a preheated air fryer at 180°C (350°F) for 5 minutes. Shake the basket, then add the tofu, spritz with oil and cook for a further 10 minutes, turning the tofu and shaking the chips halfway through.

Remove the tofu from the air fryer when crispy, increase the temperature to 200°C (400°F) and cook the chips for a further 2–3 minutes, until crispy. Serve the tofu and chips with mushy peas and lemon wedges.

For crispy nori bites with wasabi mayonnaise, wrap the tofu in the nori as above, then cut the fingers into 3.5 cm (1½ inch) pieces. Dip in the batter and coat in the breadcrumbs. Place the tofu in a preheated air fryer, spritz with oil and cook at 180°C (350°F) for 6–8 minutes, turning once, until crispy. Meanwhile, mix 50 g (2 oz) of vegan mayonnaise with 1 teaspoon of wasabi paste, or to taste. Serve the bites with the wasabi mayonnaise.

baked feta & tomato pasta

Serves **2**
Preparation time **5 minutes**
Cooking time **12 minutes**

225 g (7½ oz) **cherry tomatoes**
1 **garlic clove**, chopped
100 g (3½ oz) piece of **feta cheese**
1 tablespoon **olive oil**
pinch of **dried chilli flakes**
200 g (7 oz) **dried penne pasta**
2 tablespoons sliced **black olives** (optional)
salt and **pepper**
1 tablespoon **basil leaves**, to garnish

Arrange the tomatoes and garlic in an ovenproof dish and nestle the feta in the middle. Drizzle over the olive oil, sprinkle over the chilli flakes and season with pepper.

Place the dish in a preheated air fryer and cook at 190°C (375°F) for 10 minutes, gently shaking the tomatoes halfway through, until the feta is soft and the tomatoes have burst.

Meanwhile, cook the pasta in a saucepan of lightly salted boiling water according to the packet instructions, until just tender. Drain, reserving 2 tablespoons of the cooking water.

Stir the drained pasta into the tomatoes and feta, with the olives, if using, adding 1–2 tablespoons of the reserved water to make a creamy sauce. Divide between 2 bowls and serve immediately sprinkled with pepper and the basil leaves.

For garlic, herb, tomato & spinach spaghetti, place the tomatoes in an ovenproof dish as above, omitting the garlic, and add a 150 g (5 oz) round of garlic and herb soft cheese. Drizzle over the oil, place the dish in a preheated air fryer and cook as above, until the tomatoes have burst. Meanwhile, cook 200 g (7 oz) of dried spaghetti according to the packet instructions, until just tender. Drain, reserving 2 tablespoons of the cooking water. Stir the tomatoes and cheese together, then stir in 200 g (7 oz) of baby spinach and the drained spaghetti with a little of the pasta water. Mix well until the spinach has wilted. Serve immediately.

katsu sweet potato curry

Serves **2**
Preparation time **20 minutes**
Cooking time **25 minutes**

4 tablespoons **plain flour**
4 tablespoons **cold water**
50 g (2 oz) **panko breadcrumbs**
1 large **sweet potato**, peeled
    and cut on the diagonal into
    slices 1 cm (½ inch) thick
olive oil, for spritzing
salt and **pepper**

Katsu sauce
1 tablespoon **sunflower oil**
1 **onion**, finely chopped
2 **garlic cloves**, crushed
2.5 cm (1 inch) piece of **fresh
    root ginger**, peeled and grated
1 **carrot**, diced
1 tablespoon **mild curry powder**
1 teaspoon **ground turmeric**
1 tablespoon **plain flour**
300 ml (½ pint) **vegetable stock**
100 ml (3½ fl oz) **coconut milk**
1 teaspoon **soy sauce**
2 teaspoons **apple sauce**

To serve
steamed **rice**
salad leaves

Heat the oil for the sauce in a saucepan over a medium heat, add the onion, garlic and ginger and cook for 2 minutes, then stir in the carrot. Cover and cook over a low heat for 10 minutes, stirring occasionally, until the vegetables have softened and are starting to caramelize.

Stir in the spices and flour and cook for 2 minutes, then gradually stir in the stock. Add the coconut milk, soy and apple sauce, reduce the heat and simmer, uncovered, for 10 minutes. Season, then press the sauce through a sieve.

Place the flour in a bowl and stir in the measured water to make a smooth paste, then season with a little salt and pepper. Place the breadcrumbs on a plate. Dip each slice of sweet potato in the paste to coat and then in the breadcrumbs.

Arrange the sweet potato in a single layer in a preheated air fryer, spritz with oil and cook at 180°C (350°F) for 18–20 minutes, turning halfway through and spritzing with more oil, until the potato is tender, yet crisp on the outside. Serve with the sauce, steamed rice and salad leaves.

For piri piri sweet potatoes, prepare the sweet potatoes and make the paste as above. Mix the panko breadcrumbs with 1 tablespoon of piri piri seasoning and 2 teaspoons of finely grated lemon zest. Coat the potatoes in the paste mixture as above, then in the breadcrumbs, and cook as above. Meanwhile, in a small food processor, blitz together 4 tablespoons of chopped fresh coriander, 6 tablespoons of plant-based Greek yogurt and 1 tablespoon of lemon juice to make a green sauce. Serve the sweet potatoes with rice, with the sauce poured on top.

vegetable & chickpea tagine

Serves **4**
Preparation time **10 minutes**
Cooking time **26 minutes**

2 **parsnips**, cut into 2.5 cm
   (1 inch) chunks
2 **carrots**, cut into 2.5 cm
   (1 inch) chunks
1 **red onion**, cut into 8 wedges
2 teaspoons **olive oil**
2 teaspoons **Moroccan spice
   mix**
4 **tomatoes**, quartered
300 ml (½ pint) hot **vegetable
   stock**
2 teaspoons **harissa paste**
1 tablespoon **tomato purée**
400 g (13 oz) can **chickpeas**,
   drained and rinsed
50 g (2 oz) **pitted green olives**
6 **dried apricots**, chopped
1 **preserved lemon**, halved,
   flesh discarded and skin
   chopped
salt and **pepper**
2 tablespoons chopped **flat
   leaf parsley**, to garnish
couscous, to serve

Place the parsnips, carrots and onion in a bowl, drizzle
over the oil and sprinkle over the spice mix. Season and
toss well to coat.

Cook in a preheated air fryer at 180°C (350°F) for
14 minutes, shaking the basket halfway through and
adding the tomatoes.

Remove any crisping plates or baskets from the
air fryer, then tip the vegetables into the base and
add all the remaining ingredients. Cook for a further
12 minutes, stirring halfway through. Season to taste,
sprinkle with the parsley and serve with couscous.

For aubergine & date tagine, cut 2 aubergines into
3.5 cm (1½ inch) chunks. Omit the parsnips and toss
in a bowl with the carrots, onion, oil, spice mix and salt
and pepper. Cook as above, stirring halfway through and
adding the tomatoes. Tip into the base as above, adding
all the other ingredients but substituting the dried apricots
with 6 dried pitted dates. Cook as above.

lentil & mushroom meatless balls

Serves **4**
Preparation time **15 minutes**
Cooking time **25 minutes**

250 g (8 oz) **chestnut mushrooms**, chopped
1 **garlic clove**, crushed
1 small **onion**, roughly chopped
1 tablespoon **olive oil**
250 g (8 oz) canned **green lentils**, drained
1 tablespoon **tomato purée**
2 tablespoons chopped **flat leaf parsley**
2 teaspoons **dried mixed herbs**
2 tablespoons **dried breadcrumbs**
25 g (1 oz) **vegan Italian-style hard cheese**, grated, plus extra to serve
350 g (11½ oz) **dried spaghetti**
salt and **pepper**
basil leaves, to garnish

Tomato sauce
1 tablespoon **olive oil**
1 **garlic clove**, crushed
2 × 400 g (13 oz) cans **chopped tomatoes**
1 teaspoon **dried oregano**
1 teaspoon **sugar**

Place the mushrooms, garlic and onion in a bowl, pour over the oil and toss well. Cook in a preheated air fryer at 180°C (350°F) for 10 minutes, shaking the basket halfway through, until softened. Cool slightly, then place in a food processor and pulse until finely chopped. Add the remaining ingredients, except the spaghetti, and pulse until the mixture starts to come together. Shape the mixture into 16 balls and chill while you make the sauce.

Heat the oil in a saucepan over a medium heat, add the garlic and cook for 2–3 minutes, until softened but not browned. Stir in the tomatoes, oregano and sugar. Bring to the boil, then reduce the heat and simmer, uncovered, for 12–15 minutes, stirring occasionally.

Cook, the meatballs in a preheated air fryer at 180°C (350°F) for 10 minutes. Meanwhile, cook the pasta in a saucepan of lightly salted boiling water according to the packet instructions, until just tender. Drain well.

Divide the pasta between 4 bowls, spoon over the meatballs and sauce, sprinkle over some cheese and garnish with basil leaves.

For Moroccan-style meatless balls, cook the mushrooms, garlic and onion as above, with 2 teaspoons of ground cumin and 1 teaspoon ground cinnamon. Place in a food processor, with the lentils, tomato purée, breadcrumbs and seasoning, omitting the vegan cheese. Make and cook as above. Prepare the sauce as above, omitting the dried oregano, and stir in 2 teaspoons of harissa paste and 2 tablespoons of chopped flat leaf parsley. Serve the meatballs with couscous with the sauce poured over.

whole roasted cauliflower

Serves **3–4**

Preparation time **15 minutes, plus marinating**

Cooking time **40 minutes**

1 small **cauliflower**

½ teaspoon **ground turmeric**

½ teaspoon **salt**

Marinade

100 ml (3½ fl oz) **coconut yogurt**

2 teaspoons grated **fresh root ginger**

1 **garlic clove**, crushed

2 tablespoons **tandoori spice mix**

1 tablespoon **sunflower oil**

1 tablespoon **lemon juice**

½ teaspoon **salt**

To serve

3–4 **mini naan breads**, warmed

½ **red onion**, thinly sliced

ready-made cucumber raita

2 tablespoons chopped **fresh coriander**

Trim the leaves off the cauliflower and trim the stalk so that it sits flat. Cut a cross in the stalk. Bring a large saucepan of water to the boil and add the turmeric and salt. Gently lower in the cauliflower and simmer for 4 minutes, turning halfway through. Drain in a colander and leave to steam dry, stalk side up.

Meanwhile, mix together all the marinade ingredients in a large bowl. Add the cauliflower and coat all over on both sides. Leave to marinate for at least 30 minutes, or overnight.

Cook the cauliflower, florets side up, in a preheated air fryer at 160°C (325°F) for 30–35 minutes, until tender, then cut into pieces. Serve on the warmed naans with the red onion, raita and fresh coriander.

For za'atar-roasted cauliflower with dates & pine nuts, cut ½ head of cauliflower into 2.5 cm (1 inch) florets. Place in a bowl, drizzle over 2 teaspoons of olive oil and 1 tablespoon of za'atar spice mix and season with salt and pepper. Cook in a preheated air fryer at 180°C (350°F) for 12 minutes, shaking the basket a couple of times, until crisp. Meanwhile, make a dressing by combining 1 crushed garlic clove with 1 tablespoon of tahini, 2 teaspoons of lemon juice, 1 tablespoon of honey and 100 ml (3½ fl oz) of yogurt. Roughly chop 4 pitted dates, then serve the cauliflower on flatbreads, scattered with the dates and a handful of toasted pine nuts. Drizzle over the dressing and sprinkle with sumac.

crispy butternut squash gnocchi

Serves **2**
Preparation time **5 minutes**
Cooking time **22 minutes**

250 g (8 oz) **butternut squash**,
   peeled, deseeded and cut
   into 2.5 cm (1 inch) cubes
1 tablespoon **olive oil**
250 g (8 oz) **vegan gnocchi**
1 small **red onion**, cut into
   wedges
8 **sage leaves**
50 g (2 oz) **baby spinach**
2 tablespoons **vegan pesto**
1 tablespoon toasted **pine nuts**
salt and **pepper**

Place the butternut squash in a bowl and add
1 teaspoon of the oil. Toss with a little salt and pepper.
Cook in a preheated air fryer at 200°C (400°F) for
10 minutes, shaking the basket halfway through.

Toss the gnocchi, onion wedges and sage leaves in
the remaining oil, add to the air fryer and cook for a
further 10–12 minutes, shaking the basket a couple
of times, until the gnocchi is crispy and the squash is
tender. Add the spinach about 1 minute before the end
of the cooking time. Stir well so the spinach is all wilted.

Transfer to 2 serving plates, drizzle with the pesto and
sprinkle with a good grind of black pepper and the pine
nuts. Serve immediately.

For crispy gnocchi with roasted peppers & vegan

feta, core and deseed 1 red and 1 yellow pepper, then
cut into chunks. Place in a bowl with 6 cherry tomatoes,
the of vegan gnocchi, 1 crushed garlic clove and
2 teaspoons of olive oil. Season and toss well. Cook in a
preheated air fryer at 200°C (400°F) for 10–12 minutes,
shaking the basket halfway through, until the peppers
have softened and the gnocchi is crispy. Scatter over
125 g (4 oz) of vegan feta cheese. Transfer to 2 bowls
and serve drizzled with a little extra virgin olive oil and
a few basil leaves.

spicy bean burgers

Serves **4**

Preparation time **15 minutes**

Cooking time **30 minutes**

450 g (14½ oz) **sweet potatoes**, peeled and cut into cubes

1 teaspoon **olive oil**, plus extra for brushing

400 g (13 oz) can **black beans**, drained and rinsed

1 tablespoon **chipotle paste**

finely grated zest and juice of ½ **lime**

2 tablespoons chopped **fresh coriander**

salt and **pepper**

To serve

4 **burger buns**, halved

handful of **mixed salad leaves**

4 large slices of **tomato**

4 slices of **red onion**

4 tablespoons **vegan mayonnaise**

1 **avocado**, stoned, peeled and sliced

Toss the sweet potatoes in the oil. Cook in a preheated air fryer at 180°C (350°F) for 20 minutes, until tender. Cool slightly.

Place the black beans, sweet potato, chipotle paste, lime zest and juice, fresh coriander and a good sprinkling of salt and pepper in a food processor and pulse until the mixture is roughly combined. Shape the mixture into 4 burgers, then brush each with a little oil.

Cook the burgers in a preheated air fryer at 180°C (350°F) for 10 minutes, turning halfway through.

Grill the buns until lightly toasted, then top each base with some salad leaves and a slice of tomato and onion. Add the burgers and serve topped with the mayonnaise, avocado slices and bun tops.

For spicy bean balls, prepare the mixture as above and shape into 14–16 balls. Place in a preheated air fryer, spritz with a little sunflower oil and cook at 180°C (350°F) for 10 minutes. Meanwhile, place 500 ml (17 fl oz) of passata (sieved tomatoes) in a saucepan, stir in 1 teaspoon each of dried oregano, salt and granulated sugar, cover and simmer for 5 minutes. Serve the bean balls on rice with the sauce poured over, with a dollop of soured cream on the side.

roasted balsamic veg & halloumi

Serves **2**
Preparation time **5 minutes**
Cooking time **20 minutes**

1 **red** or **yellow pepper**,
deseeded and cut into chunks
1 **courgette**, thickly sliced
1 **red onion**, cut into 8 wedges
2 **garlic cloves**, peeled
2 teaspoons **olive oil**
2 teaspoons **balsamic vinegar**
1 teaspoon **Italian dried mixed herbs**
8 **baby plum** or **cherry tomatoes**
125 g (4 oz) **halloumi cheese**, cut into 6 slices
salt and **pepper**
ciabatta bread, to serve

Place the red or yellow pepper, courgette and onion wedges in a bowl, add the garlic, oil, vinegar and dried herbs and season well, then toss to coat. Cook in a preheated air fryer at 180°C (350°F) for 12 minutes.

Stir the vegetables gently, then add the tomatoes and arrange the halloumi slices on top. Cook for a further 6–8 minutes, until the tomatoes have softened and the cheese is golden.

Divide between 2 plates, drizzle with any juices from the bottom of the air fryer and serve with warm ciabatta bread.

For halloumi traybake with honey & chilli drizzle,
prepare and cook the vegetables and halloumi as above, omitting the vinegar. Meanwhile, mix 1 tablespoon of honey with a pinch of dried chilli flakes and 1 teaspoon of extra virgin olive oil. Divide the vegetables and halloumi between 2 plates and drizzle over the honey and chilli mixture to serve.

miso-glazed aubergines

Serves **2**
Preparation time **5 minutes**
Cooking time **24 minutes**

2 small **aubergines**
2 tablespoons **sunflower oil**
4 tablespoons **white miso paste**
2 tablespoons **rice wine vinegar** or **mirin**
2 tablespoons **sake** or **water**
1 tablespoon **caster sugar**
1 tablespoon toasted **black and white sesame seeds**
2 **spring onions**, thinly sliced
steamed **jasmine rice**, to serve

Cut the aubergines in half lengthways, then score the cut sides of the flesh in a diamond pattern, being careful not to cut all the way through. Brush the flesh of each aubergine with the oil, then cook, cut sides up, in a preheated air fryer at 190°C (375°F) for 12 minutes, until softened.

Mix together the miso paste, rice wine vinegar, sake and sugar in a small bowl. Brush the aubergines with half the miso glaze and cook for a further 12 minutes, brushing with the remaining glaze halfway through, until softened, sticky and caramelized. Sprinkle with the sesame seeds and spring onions and serve with steamed jasmine rice.

For miso-roasted vegetables, cut 2 sweet potatoes and 1 courgette into 2.5 cm (1 inch) pieces. Place in a bowl with 1 red onion, cut into wedges, and stir in 1 tablespoon of white miso paste, 2 teaspoons of sunflower oil and 2 tablespoons of water. Season and cook in a preheated air fryer at 180°C (350°F) for 18–20 minutes, stirring halfway through, until the vegetables are tender. Serve scattered with chopped spring onions and toasted sesame seeds.

meat &
fish mains

chicken wrapped in parma ham

Serves **4**

Preparation time **10 minutes**

Cooking time **20 minutes**

1 **lemon**

8 slices of **Parma ham** or **prosciutto**

4 **boneless, skinless chicken breasts**

12 **sage leaves**

pepper

To serve

new potatoes

asparagus

Grate the zest from the lemon, then cut it in half. Lay out 2 slices of the ham on a chopping board, slightly overlapping. Place a chicken breast on top and arrange 3 sage leaves across the top. Sprinkle over some of the lemon zest, then season with pepper. Wrap the ham around the chicken to fully enclose, then repeat with the remaining ingredients.

Cook the chicken in a preheated air fryer at 180°C (350°F) for 18–20 minutes, until the ham is crispy and the chicken cooked through, adding the lemon halves for the last 6 minutes of the cooking time.

Serve the chicken, sliced, with new potatoes and asparagus, with the lemon squeezed over the top.

For garlic & herb chicken, use a sharp knife to carefully cut a pocket in the side of each chicken breast, starting on the long side and working your way through the chicken almost to the other side. Open the pockets and spoon 25 g (1 oz) of garlic and herb soft cheese into each. Close the pockets and season with pepper. Wrap each breast in 1 slice of Parma ham or prosciutto, ensuring the ham covers the opening of the pocket to help keep the cheese sealed inside. Cook as above.

paprika pork goujons & fries

Serves **2**
Preparation time **10 minutes**
Cooking time **26 minutes**

200 g (7 oz) **frozen French fries**
2 **pork loin steaks**, trimmed of any fat
50 g (2 oz) **fine dried breadcrumbs**
finely grated zest of **1 lemon**
1 teaspoon **dried mixed herbs**
2 teaspoons **paprika**
1 teaspoon **garlic powder**
1 tablespoon **plain flour**
1 **egg**, beaten
sunflower oil, for spritzing
salt and **pepper**

Lemon mayonnaise
2 tablespoons **mayonnaise**
1 tablespoon **lemon juice**

Cook the fries in a preheated air fryer at 180°C (350°F) for 18 minutes, shaking the basket a few times during cooking. Meanwhile, place the pork between 2 pieces of baking paper and bash with a rolling pin to about 1 cm (½ inch) thick, then cut into 2.5 cm (1 inch) wide goujons.

Place the breadcrumbs, lemon zest, herbs, paprika and garlic powder in a bowl, season with salt and pepper and mix together. Sprinkle the flour on a plate and season to taste. Coat the pork goujons in the seasoned flour, dip in the egg, then coat in the breadcrumbs.

Remove the fries to a bowl. Place the goujons in a single layer in the air fryer, spritz with oil and cook for 6 minutes, turning halfway, until cooked through. Remove the pork, return the fries to the air fryer and cook for a further 2 minutes, until crispy and heated through.

Mix the mayonnaise with the lemon juice and serve with the goujons and fries.

For lemon & Parmesan pork schnitzels, place the pork steaks in a plastic bag and bash with a rolling pin until 5 mm (¼ inch) thick. In a bowl, mix together the fine dried breadcrumbs, 25 g (1 oz) of grated Parmesan, 1 teaspoon of ground pepper and the grated lemon zest and place on a plate. Beat 1 egg in a bowl and place 4 tablespoons of seasoned flour on a plate. Coat the pork in the flour, then the egg, then the breadcrumbs. Place in a preheated air fryer, spritz with oil and cook at 180°C (350°F) for 8–9 minutes, turning halfway through, until the crumb is crisp and the pork cooked through.

pineapple & piri piri turkey burgers

Serves **4**
Preparation time **10 minutes**
Cooking time **20 minutes**

4 **brioche burger buns**, halved
sunflower oil, for spritzing
4 canned **pineapple rings**, drained
4 tablespoons **light mayonnaise**
2 tablespoons **piri piri sauce**
4 **round lettuce leaves**
8 **red onion** rings

Piri piri burgers
500 g (1 lb) **minced turkey**
1 bunch of **spring onions**, finely chopped
2 tablespoons **piri piri seasoning**
finely grated zest and juice of 1 **lemon**
salt and **pepper**

Place all the burger ingredients in a large bowl and mix until well combined. Shape the mixture into 4 burgers.

Arrange the burger buns, cut sides down, in a preheated air fryer and cook at 200°C (400°F) for 1–2 minutes, until the buns are lightly toasted, then remove the buns. You may need to do this in 2 batches.

Place the burgers in the preheated air fryer, spritz with a little oil and cook at 180°C (350°F) for 14–16 minutes, turning halfway through, until the juices run clear.

Remove the burgers, increase the temperature to 200°C (400°F) and cook the pineapple rings for 2–3 minutes, turning once, until starting to caramelize.

Mix the mayonnaise with the piri piri sauce and spread over the bun bases. Top each with a lettuce leaf, burger, pineapple ring and 2 slices of onion. Add the lids and serve immediately.

For tikka turkey burgers, place the turkey mince in a bowl with 1 finely chopped red onion, 4 tablespoons of tikka paste, 2 tablespoons of natural yogurt, the finely grated zest of 1 lemon, 1 tablespoon of lemon juice and 2 tablespoons of chopped fresh coriander. Season with salt and pepper, mix well and shape into 4 burgers. Cook as above and serve on mini naan breads with crispy salad leaves, sliced tomatoes and mango chutney.

chicken gyros

Serves **4**

Preparation time **15 minutes, plus marinating**

Cooking time **12 minutes**

250 g (8 oz) **skinless chicken breast** or **thigh**, cut into 1.5 cm (¾ inch) thick pieces

4 **flatbreads**

8 **cherry tomatoes**, halved

large handful of **crispy lettuce**, shredded

½ small **red onion**, thinly sliced

4 **lemon wedges**

Marinade

2 teaspoons **olive oil**

1 tablespoon **lemon juice**

1 **garlic clove**, crushed

1 teaspoon **dried oregano**

½ teaspoon **dried thyme**

½ teaspoon **smoked paprika**

½ teaspoon **ground cumin**

Tzatziki

7 cm (3 inch) piece of **cucumber**, grated

½ teaspoon **salt**

100 ml (3½ fl oz) **Greek yogurt**

1 tablespoon chopped **dill**

1 teaspoon **lemon juice**

1 **garlic clove**, crushed

Mix together all the marinade ingredients and stir in the chicken. Cover and leave to marinate in the refrigerator for at least 30 minutes.

Make the tzatziki by placing the grated cucumber in a sieve set over a bowl. Stir in the salt and leave for 30 minutes, then squeeze any excess moisture out of the cucumber and pat dry on kitchen paper. Place all the remaining sauce ingredients in a bowl and stir in the cucumber.

Thread the chicken on to 4 small metal skewers, or 4 wooden skewers that have been soaked in water to prevent them burning. Cook in a preheated air fryer at 180°C (350°F) for 10–12 minutes, until the chicken is cooked through.

Warm the flatbreads and top with the tomatoes, lettuce and onion. Add the chicken and top with the tzatziki. Squeeze over the lemon and serve immediately.

For satay chicken skewers, place 2 teaspoons of ground coriander, 1 teaspoon each of ground cumin and ground turmeric, 2 teaspoons of sunflower oil, 2 teaspoons of grated fresh root ginger and 1 tablespoon of dark soy sauce in a bowl. Stir in the chicken pieces, cover and leave to marinate for at least 1 hour. Thread on to 8 small skewers and cook as above. Make a peanut sauce by placing 3 tablespoons of crunchy peanut butter in a pan with the juice of 1 lime, 1 tablespoon of soy sauce, ½ teaspoon of hot chilli powder and 2 tablespoons of water. Cook over a medium heat, stirring, until the ingredients are combined. Cool slightly, then serve with the skewers.

smoked haddock fishcakes

Serves **4**

Preparation time **20 minutes, plus cooling and chilling**

Cooking time **30 minutes**

375 g (12 oz) **floury potatoes**, peeled and chopped

knob of **butter**

sunflower oil, for brushing and spritzing

325 g (11 oz) **boneless, skinless smoked haddock**

3 tablespoons **plain flour**

1 **egg**, beaten

75 g (3 oz) **fine dried breadcrumbs**

salt and **pepper**

Sauce

15 g (½ oz) **butter**

15 g (½ oz) **plain flour**

150 ml (¼ pint) **milk**

½ teaspoon **Dijon mustard**

25 g (1 oz) **Parmesan cheese**, grated

2 tablespoons chopped **parsley**

To serve

peas

4 **lemon wedges**

128

Cook the potatoes in a saucepan of lightly salted boiling water for 15 minutes, until tender. Drain, return to the pan, mash with the butter and season to taste. Transfer to a bowl and leave to cool. Meanwhile, brush a piece of foil with a little oil, wrap the fish in the foil and cook in a preheated air fryer at 180°C (350°F) for 7–10 minutes, until flaky. Remove and leave to cool.

Place the butter, flour and milk for the sauce in a small saucepan over a medium heat and whisk continuously for 2–3 minutes, until smooth and thick. Add the mustard, Parmesan and parsley, stir until the cheese has melted and season to taste. Transfer to a bowl and leave to cool.

Flake the fish and stir into the potatoes. Divide the mixture into 4 balls. Press your thumb into the middle of one to make a well, then fill with some of the sauce. Remould the top so the sauce is enclosed, then flatten slightly into a fishcake. Repeat with the remaining mixture.

Dust each fishcake lightly in the flour. Coat in the beaten egg, then coat in the breadcrumbs. Transfer to a plate, cover and chill in the refrigerator for 30 minutes (or up to a day ahead).

Place the fishcakes in a preheated air fryer, spritz with a little oil and cook at 180°C (350°F) for 13–15 minutes, turning halfway through and spritzing with more oil, until golden and crispy. Serve with peas and a lemon wedge.

For salmon fishcakes, prepare as above, substituting the smoked haddock with salmon. Make the sauce, omitting the mustard and cheese. Assemble and cook as above.

steak with blue cheese butter

Serves **2**

Preparation time **5 minutes,**
    plus chilling

Cooking time **10 minutes**

2 x 225 g (7½ oz) **sirloin**
    steaks, at room temperature

2 teaspoons **olive oil**

salt and **pepper**

Blue cheese butter

25 g (1 oz) **butter**, softened

25 g (1 oz) **blue cheese**

1 tablespoon chopped **chives**

1 tablespoon chopped **flat leaf**
    parsley

1 teaspoon coarsely crushed
    black pepper

To serve

chips or **new potatoes**

Tenderstem broccoli

Place the butter and blue cheese in a small bowl and mash together with a fork, then stir in the herbs and black pepper. Roll into a log in a piece of clingfilm and chill in the refrigerator for 30 minutes.

Brush the steaks with the oil and season with salt and pepper. Place the steaks in a preheated air fryer and cook at 200°C (400°F) for 8–10 minutes, turning halfway through, for medium steak.

Slice the butter into rounds and serve on top of the steaks with chips or new potatoes and Tenderstem broccoli. Any leftover butter can be frozen.

For horseradish, black pepper & chive butter, in place of the blue cheese butter, mix the softened butter with 2 teaspoons of horseradish cream, ½ teaspoon of coarsely crushed black pepper and 1 tablespoon of chopped chives.

southern-style chicken nuggets

Serves **2–3**

Preparation time **10 minutes, plus soaking**

Cooking time **10 minutes**

100 ml (3½ fl oz) **buttermilk**

400 g (13 oz) **chicken mini-fillets**, each cut into 3 pieces

Southern-style coating

50 g (2 oz) **fine dried breadcrumbs**

1 teaspoon **garlic powder**

1 teaspoon **onion powder**

2 teaspoons **smoked paprika**

1 teaspoon freshly ground **black pepper**

1 teaspoon **dried thyme**

1 teaspoon **dried oregano**

½ teaspoon **salt**

To serve

chips

coleslaw

Place the buttermilk in a bowl, add the chicken pieces, stir to coat and set aside to soak for 10 minutes.

Mix all the coating ingredients in a bowl until well combined. Dip each piece of chicken in the crumb mixture until fully coated, then place on a plate.

Cook the chicken nuggets in a single layer in a preheated air fryer at 190°C (375°F) for 10 minutes, turning halfway through, until crispy and cooked through. You may need to do this in 2 batches. Serve with chips and coleslaw.

For Mediterranean nuggets, mix the breadcrumbs with 25 g (1 oz) of freshly grated Parmesan and 2 teaspoons of dried mixed herbs, then season to taste. Place 125 ml (4 fl oz) of ready-made pizza sauce or tomato pasta sauce in a bowl. Dip each chicken piece in the sauce to coat, then roll in the breadcrumbs. Cook as above and serve with a little extra warmed pizza or pasta sauce, for dipping.

fish tacos with pickled radishes

Serves **4**

Preparation time **20 minutes**

Cooking time **6 minutes**

6 **radishes**, thinly sliced

juice of 2½ **limes**

75 g (3 oz) **mayonnaise**

1–2 teaspoons **chilli paste**

2 ripe **avocados**

500 g (1 lb) **cod** or **haddock loin**, cut into pieces about 2.5 x 5 cm (1 x 2 inches)

sunflower oil, for spritzing

8 **mini corn** or **wheat tortillas**, warmed

2 **Little Gem lettuces**, shredded

2 tablespoons **fresh coriander leaves**

salt and **pepper**

Fish coating

1 teaspoon **ground cumin**

½ teaspoon **hot chilli powder**

1 teaspoon **smoked paprika**

½ teaspoon **garlic powder**

½ teaspoon **salt**

finely grated zest of 1 **lime**

Place the radishes in a bowl, add the juice of 1 lime and set aside. Mix the mayonnaise in another bowl with the juice of ½ lime and the chilli paste and set aside. Cut the avocados in half, remove the stones and scoop the flesh into a third bowl. Add the juice of 1 lime, season to taste and mash well.

Mix together all the coating ingredients in a large bowl, add the fish and stir gently to coat. Place the fish in a single layer on a piece of pierced nonstick baking paper, spritz with a little oil and cook in a preheated air fryer at 190°C (375°F) for 6 minutes, turning halfway through, until the fish flakes. You may need to do this in 2 batches.

Drain the pickled radishes. Pile the warmed tortillas with some shredded lettuce, the fish, spicy mayonnaise, mashed avocado and the pickled radishes. Sprinkle over the coriander leaves and serve immediately.

For easy fish finger tacos, cook 8 frozen fish fingers in a preheated air fryer at 200°C (400°F) for 8–10 minutes, turning once, until crispy and cooked through. Serve in 8 hard taco shells stuffed with shredded lettuce, ready-made guacamole and tomato salsa, with a squeeze of lime juice.

lamb chops with mint pesto

Serves **2**
Preparation time **10 minutes**
Cooking time **22 minutes**

200 g (7 oz) small **new
potatoes,** halved if large
1 **red onion**, cut into 8 wedges
1 small **courgette**, chopped
1 teaspoon **olive oil**
4 **lamb chops**
salt and **pepper**

Mint pesto
1 **garlic clove**, peeled
25 g (1 oz) **mint leaves**
50 g (2 oz) **pea shoots**, plus
extra to serve
25 g (1 oz) **pine nuts**
25 g (1 oz) **Parmesan cheese**,
grated
4 tablespoons **extra virgin
olive oil**

Place the potatoes, onion and courgette in a bowl, drizzle over the olive oil, season with a little salt and pepper and toss to coat evenly. Season the chops.

Cook the vegetables in a preheated air fryer at 180°C (350°F) for 10 minutes, shaking the basket halfway through.

Meanwhile, make the pesto. Place the garlic, mint, pea shoots, pine nuts and Parmesan in a small food processor and blitz until smooth. Add the oil and a little water if you want a runnier consistency and season to taste.

Add the lamb chops to the air fryer and cook for 10–12 minutes more, turning halfway through and stirring the vegetables, until the lamb chops are cooked through.

Serve the chops on top of the vegetables, scatter over a few extra pea shoots and spoon over the pesto.

For lamb chops with anchovy, rosemary & garlic,
place 2 anchovy fillets from a jar in a mortar with 2 teaspoons of olive oil, 2 crushed garlic cloves and 1 tablespoon of finely chopped rosemary. Season, then pound with a pestle to make a paste. Spread over the lamb chops and leave to marinate for about 30 minutes. Cook the chops in a preheated air fryer at 180°C (350°F) for 10–12 minutes, then serve with new potatoes and Tenderstem broccoli.

herby roast chicken with lemon

Serves **3–4**

Preparation time **5 minutes, plus resting**

Cooking time **45 minutes**

1 **lemon**

2 tablespoons **sunflower oil**

1 teaspoon **paprika**

1 teaspoon **garlic powder**

2 teaspoons **dried mixed herbs**

1 teaspoon **sea salt**

1.5 kg (3 lb) **whole chicken**

pepper

roast potatoes, to serve

Grate the zest from the lemon and cut the lemon in half. Place the lemon zest in a bowl with the oil, paprika, garlic powder, dried herbs, sea salt and pepper. Brush the flavoured oil all over the chicken, then place the lemon halves in the cavity.

Cook the chicken, breast side down, in a preheated air fryer at 180°C (350°F) for 30 minutes (if the chicken touches the heating element, remove the plate). Turn the chicken over and cook for a further 15 minutes, until the skin is browned and crispy and the juices run clear when a skewer is inserted into the thickest part.

Allow the chicken to rest for 10 minutes before carving. The juices in the bottom of the air fryer can be used to make gravy, if you like. Serve with roast potatoes.

For chipotle & lime roast chicken, mix 1 tablespoon of chipotle paste with 2 tablespoons of softened butter, the finely grated zest and juice of 1 lime, 1 crushed garlic clove and 1 tablespoon of chopped fresh coriander. Using your fingers, carefully lift the chicken skin away from the meat, then spread the butter mixture under the skin. Place the squeezed lime halves in the cavity and roast as above.

soy, lime & ginger salmon

Serves **4**

Preparation time **5 minutes,**
plus marinating

Cooking time **10 minutes**

3 tablespoons **dark soy sauce**

1 tablespoon **honey**

1 **garlic clove**, crushed

2.5 cm (1 inch) piece of **fresh**
root ginger, peeled and finely
grated

2 teaspoons **sriracha chilli**
sauce

finely grated zest and juice of
1 lime

4 **skin-on salmon fillets**, about
150 g (5 oz) each

To serve

steamed **rice**

stir-fried **vegetables**

Place all the ingredients, except the salmon, in a shallow
bowl and stir well. Add the salmon fillets and turn to coat.
Leave to marinate for 10 minutes.

Arrange the salmon fillets, skin side down, in a preheated
air fryer, baste with the marinade and cook at 180°C
(350°F) for 9–10 minutes, basting again halfway through,
until the salmon is cooked through and flakes easily.
Serve with rice and a selection of stir-fried vegetables.

For salmon with crispy pesto & olive crumb, mix
3 tablespoons of basil pesto in a bowl with 8 chopped
pitted green olives, the finely grated zest of 1 lemon
and 75 g (3 oz) of fresh breadcrumbs. Press the mixture
over the top of the salmon fillets and cook, skin side down,
as above, until the salmon is cooked through. Serve with
pasta and lemon wedges.

honey mustard sausages & apples

Serves **2**
Preparation time **10 minutes**
Cooking time **24 minutes**

1 **potato**, scrubbed and cut into
  3.5 cm (1 ½ inch) pieces
1 **red onion**, cut into 8 wedges
2 teaspoons **olive oil**
2 teaspoons **wholegrain
  mustard**
2 teaspoons **honey**
4 **pork sausages**
1 **red apple**, cored and cut into
  8 wedges
6–8 **sage leaves**
salt and **pepper**

Toss the potato and onion in a bowl with the oil and season well with salt and pepper. Cook in a preheated air fryer at 180°C (350°F) for 10 minutes, shaking the basket halfway through.

Meanwhile, mix the mustard and honey in a large bowl, add the sausages and turn to coat. Add the sausages to the air fryer and continue cooking for a further 6 minutes.

Turn the sausages and stir the potato and onion. Add the apple, spoon over any remaining honey mustard mixture and scatter in the sage leaves. Cook for a further 7–8 minutes, until the sausages are sticky and browned and the potatoes and apples are tender. Serve immediately with green beans, if you like.

For sausages with sundried tomato-roasted vegetables, place the red onion wedges in a bowl with ½ chopped red pepper, ½ chopped yellow pepper and 1 chopped courgette. Stir in 2 tablespoons of sundried tomato pesto and transfer to an ovenproof dish. Place the dish in a preheated air fryer and cook at 180°C (350°F) for 10 minutes. Add the sausages, turn to coat, then cook for a further 6 minutes. Stir the vegetables and turn the sausages, then cook for a further 7–8 minutes, until the sausages are cooked through. Serve with crusty bread.

pomegranate & harissa chicken

Serves **3–4**
Preparation time **5 minutes,**
   plus marinating
Cooking time **30 minutes**

3 tablespoons **pomegranate**
   molasses or **honey**
2 teaspoons **harissa paste**
1 tablespoon **lemon juice**
½ teaspoon **ground cinnamon**
2 teaspoons **olive oil**
1 tablespoon **za'atar**
4–6 **bone-in, skin-on chicken**
   thighs
salt and **pepper**

To serve
mixed grains
50 g (2 oz) **pomegranate**
   seeds
2 tablespoons chopped **mint**
2 tablespoons chopped **flat**
   leaf parsley

Place the pomegranate molasses in a large shallow dish with the harissa paste, lemon juice, cinnamon, olive oil, za'atar and salt and pepper. Mix well, then add the chicken thighs, turn to coat and leave to marinate for at least 30 minutes.

Cook the chicken thighs, skin side down, in a preheated air fryer at 180°C (350°F) for 15 minutes. Turn, then cook for a further 10–15 minutes, until the chicken is cooked through and the skin is crispy.

Serve immediately on a bed of mixed grains, sprinkled with the pomegranate seeds and herbs, with any juices from the bottom of the air fryer spooned over.

For chicken tikka thighs, mix 100 ml (3½ fl oz) of Greek yogurt with 2 teaspoons of grated fresh root ginger, 1 crushed garlic clove, the finely grated zest and juice of ½ lemon, 1 tablespoon of mango chutney and 2 tablespoons of tikka paste. Add the chicken thighs and leave to marinate in the refrigerator for 1 hour or overnight. Cook as above and serve with steamed rice, sprinkled with chopped fresh coriander.

roast beef with a tangy crust

Serves **4**

Preparation time **5 minutes, plus resting**

Cooking time **45 minutes**

1 tablespoon **horseradish sauce**, plus extra to serve

1 tablespoon **Dijon mustard**

1 teaspoon **onion powder**

4 tablespoons **fresh breadcrumbs**

2 teaspoons chopped **thyme leaves**, plus extra sprigs to garnish

1 kg (2 lb) **boneless beef roasting joint**

olive oil, for spritzing

salt and **pepper**

Mix the horseradish in a bowl with the mustard and onion powder and season generously with salt and pepper. In a separate bowl, mix together the breadcrumbs and thyme. Spread the horseradish and mustard mixture all over the beef, then press the breadcrumbs all over to coat.

Place the joint in a preheated air fryer, spritz with oil and cook at 200°C (400°F) for 5 minutes. Reduce the temperature to 180°C (350°F) and cook for a further 35–40 minutes, turning the beef halfway through. If you prefer well-done beef, add a further 10 minutes to the cooking time.

Remove from the air fryer, cover with foil and allow to rest for 10 minutes before carving. Serve garnished with thyme sprigs with air fryer roast potatoes and your favourite vegetables, if you like, plus extra horseradish sauce.

For roast beef with herb & pepper coating, mix 1 teaspoon of sea salt with 2 tablespoons of crushed mixed peppercorns, 1 tablespoon each of chopped rosemary and flat leaf parsley, 1 crushed garlic clove and 1 tablespoon of olive oil. Rub all over the beef and cook as above.

turmeric & ginger cod

Serves **4**
Preparation time **15 minutes**
Cooking time **11 minutes**

1 **garlic clove**, crushed
1 **lemon grass stalk**, outer
leaves discarded, finely
chopped
1 teaspoon **ground turmeric**
1 tablespoon grated **fresh root
ginger**
1 tablespoon **Thai fish sauce**
2 teaspoons **light soft brown
sugar**
4 **skinless cod fillets**, about
150 g (5 oz) each
200 g (7 oz) **dried rice noodles**
2 **carrots**, thinly sliced
½ **cucumber**, thinly sliced
4 **spring onions**, thinly sliced
2 tablespoons chopped **mint**
25 g (1 oz) **roasted peanuts**,
roughly chopped
1 tablespoon **ready-made
crispy shallots**
salt

Sauce
4 tablespoons **sweet chilli
sauce**
juice of 1 **lime**
2 teaspoons **Thai fish sauce**

Place the garlic, lemon grass, turmeric, ginger, fish sauce and sugar in a bowl, stir well, then add the cod. Spoon the mixture all over the cod to coat and set aside.

Meanwhile, cook the noodles in a saucepan of lightly salted boiling water according to the packet instructions, drain and refresh under cold water. Place in a bowl and toss through the carrots, cucumber, spring onions and mint. Mix the sauce ingredients together in a small bowl.

Cook the cod in a preheated air fryer at 180°C (350°F) for 6–8 minutes, until the fish is cooked through and flakes easily. Divide the noodles between 4 plates and spoon over the sauce. Top with the cod and scatter with chopped peanuts and crispy shallots.

For coconut & lime cod, mix 4 tablespoons of coconut cream with the finely grated zest and juice of 1 lime, 2 teaspoons of grated fresh root ginger and 1 tablespoon of Thai red curry paste. Add the cod and turn to coat. Cook the cod as above and serve with Thai steamed rice and sugar snaps.

chicken kiev with a twist

Serves **2**
Preparation time **20 minutes**
Cooking time **15 minutes**

4 tablespoons **butter**, softened
1 **garlic clove**, crushed
4 tablespoons chopped **fresh coriander**
1 small **red chilli**, deseeded and finely chopped
finely grated zest of **1 lime**
2 **boneless, skinless chicken breasts**
2 tablespoons **plain flour**
1 large **egg**, beaten
75 g (3 oz) **panko breadcrumbs**
sunflower oil, for spritzing
salt and **pepper**

To serve
new potatoes
Tenderstem broccoli

Place the butter in a bowl with the garlic, fresh coriander, chilli and lime zest, season well and mash with a fork until combined. Chill in the refrigerator while you prepare the chicken.

Use a sharp knife to make a pocket in the side of each chicken breast, starting at the thick end and being careful not to cut all the way through. Fill with the chilled butter and press to seal.

Sprinkle the flour on a plate and season with salt and pepper, then place the egg and breadcrumbs in 2 separate shallow bowls. Dust the chicken with the flour, then dip in the beaten egg, followed by the breadcrumbs, making sure it is well coated. Repeat with the egg, then the breadcrumbs, to double coat.

Place the chicken in a preheated air fryer, spritz with oil and cook at 180°C (350°F) for 12–15 minutes, until the crumb is crispy and the chicken is cooked through. Serve immediately with new potatoes and Tenderstem broccoli.

For garlic & parsley Kievs, mix 4 tablespoons of softened butter with 1 large crushed garlic clove and 4 tablespoons of chopped flat leaf parsley. Season with salt and pepper and use to fill the chicken breasts as above. Coat and cook as above.

sides

flatbreads

Makes **4**
Preparation time **5 minutes**
Cooking time **6 minutes**

150 g (5 oz) **self-raising
   flour**, plus extra for dusting
¼ teaspoon **salt**
150 g (5 oz) **natural yogurt**
olive oil, for spritzing

Place the flour and salt in a bowl. Add the yogurt and stir in with a spoon until roughly combined. Then, using clean hands, bring everything together to a make a rough dough. Knead the mixture on a lightly floured surface for 1–2 minutes, until the dough is smooth.

Cut the dough into 4 pieces and shape into rounds. Roll out each into an oval shape about 2.5 mm (⅛ inch) thick.

Spritz each with a little oil, then cook in a single layer in a preheated air fryer at 200°C (400°F) for 6 minutes, until golden brown and slightly puffed. You may need to do this in 2 batches.

For garlic & sesame seed flatbreads, stir 2 tablespoons of sesame seeds into the flour and salt. Prepare and cook the flatbreads as above, then brush the hot flatbreads with melted garlic butter before serving.

polenta, rosemary & cheese fries

Serves **4–6**

Preparation time **10 minutes, plus cooling and chilling**

Cooking time **15 minutes**

olive oil, for greasing and spritzing

800 ml (1 pint 7 fl oz) hot **vegetable stock**

1 tablespoon chopped **rosemary**

200 g (7 oz) **quick-cook polenta**

50 g (2 oz) grated **Parmesan** or **vegan hard cheese**

3 tablespoons **cornflour**

pepper

Grease a 20 cm (8 inch) square cake tin. Place the stock and rosemary in a saucepan over a medium heat and season with pepper. Add the polenta and stir continuously for 5 minutes, until thick. Remove from the heat and stir in the Parmesan.

Spoon into the prepared tin and smooth the top with a spatula. Leave to cool, then chill in the refrigerator for 2 hours.

Transfer the polenta to a chopping board when ready to serve. Cut into fries about 7.5 x 1.5 cm (3 x ¾ inches). Roll the fries in the cornflour and shake off any excess.

Place in a single layer in a preheated air fryer, spritz with oil and cook at 200°C (400°F) for 10 minutes, turning halfway through and spritzing with a little more oil, until the fries are golden and crisp. You may need to do this in 2 batches. Serve immediately, seasoned with black pepper.

For courgette & Parmesan fries, cut 1 courgette into fries about 1.5 cm (¾ inch) thick and 5 cm (2 inches) long. Place 2 tablespoons of flour on a plate and season with salt and pepper. Break 1 large egg into a bowl and beat lightly, then mix 40 g (1 ½ oz) of dried panko breadcrumbs with 25 g (1 oz) of grated Parmesan on another plate. Dip the courgettes in the flour, then the egg, then the breadcrumb mixture. Place in a single layer in a preheated air fryer, spritz with oil and cook at 190°C (375°F) for 10–12 minutes, turning halfway through, until golden. Serves 2–3.

parmesan & thyme mushrooms

Serves **2–3**
Preparation time **8 minutes**
Cooking time **10 minutes**

25 g (1 oz) **plain flour**
½ teaspoon **garlic powder**
200 g (7 oz) **button mushrooms**, wiped
1 **egg**, beaten
25 g (1 oz) **panko breadcrumbs**
15 g (½ oz) **Parmesan cheese**, grated
2 teaspoons chopped **thyme leaves**
olive oil, for spritzing
salt and **pepper**

Stir together the flour, garlic powder and salt and pepper in a bowl. Add the mushrooms and toss to coat.

Place the beaten egg in one bowl and in another bowl, mix together the breadcrumbs, Parmesan and thyme. Dip the mushrooms in the egg and then in the crumbs to coat all over.

Arrange in a preheated air fryer, spritz with oil and cook at 190°C (375°F) for 8–10 minutes, shaking the basket once, until crispy. Serve immediately.

For garlic mushrooms, place the button mushrooms in a bowl, drizzle over 2 teaspoons of olive oil, 1 teaspoon of soy sauce and 1 crushed garlic clove and toss well. Cook as above, then serve sprinkled with 2 tablespoons of chopped flat leaf parsley.

flavour-bomb potatoes

Serves **4**
Preparation time **10 minutes**
Cooking time **20 minutes**

550 g (1 lb 2 oz) **potatoes**,
   peeled and cut into 2 cm
   (¾ inch) pieces
1 tablespoon **sunflower oil**
1 tablespoon grated **fresh root**
   ginger
1 teaspoon **cumin seeds**
1 teaspoon **garlic powder**
1 teaspoon **onion powder**
1 teaspoon **black mustard**
   seeds
½ teaspoon **ground turmeric**
2 teaspoons **ground coriander**
1 teaspoon **garam masala**
1 teaspoon **hot chilli powder**
2 **tomatoes**, roughly chopped
½ teaspoon **salt**
pepper
large handful of chopped **fresh**
   coriander, to garnish

Place the potatoes in a large bowl, add all the remaining ingredients, except the fresh coriander, and stir well to coat.

Cook in a preheated air fryer at 190°C (375°F) for 20 minutes, shaking halfway through, until the potatoes are tender. Serve sprinkled with the fresh coriander.

For patatas bravas, toss 750 g (1 ½ lb) of chopped potatoes with 1 tablespoon of olive oil and ½ teaspoon of salt. Cook in a preheated air fryer at 200°C (400°F) for 20 minutes, shaking once, until crisp and golden. Make a sauce by heating 2 tablespoons of olive oil in a frying pan over a low heat and cooking 1 small chopped onion for 5 minutes, until softened. Add 2 crushed garlic cloves, 1 deseeded and finely chopped red chilli, 250 g (8 oz) of canned chopped tomatoes, 1 tablespoon of tomato purée, 2 teaspoons of hot smoked paprika, a pinch of sugar and 1 tablespoon of sherry vinegar. Season, then bring to the boil, stirring occasionally. Reduce the heat and simmer for 10 minutes, until pulpy. Tip the potatoes into serving dishes, spoon over the tomato sauce and sprinkle with chopped flat leaf parsley.

yorkshire puddings

Makes **4**
Preparation time **5 minutes**
Cooking time **25 minutes**

50 g (2 oz) **plain flour**
pinch of **salt**
4 tablespoons **milk**
4 tablespoons **water**
1 large **egg**
2 teaspoons **sunflower oil**

Place the flour and salt in a bowl and mix together the milk and measured water in a jug. Using a whisk, gradually add the egg and a little of the milk mixture to the flour, whisking to incorporate, then add the remaining liquid, until you have a smooth batter. Transfer the mixture to a jug.

Divide the oil between 4 metal pudding tins or ramekins, about 150 ml (¼ pint) capacity each, then brush it up the sides. Place the tins in a preheated air fryer at 200°C (400°F) for 5 minutes to heat.

Pour the mixture into the tins and cook for 20 minutes, without opening the drawer. The Yorkshires will be risen and golden brown. Serve immediately.

For mustard & herb Yorkshires, stir 1 tablespoon of mustard powder and 1 tablespoon of chopped thyme and rosemary into the flour and salt. Make and cook the Yorkshire puddings as above.

perfect roast potatoes

Serves **4**

Preparation time **10 minutes**

Cooking time **27 minutes**

1 kg (2 lb) **floury potatoes**,
  such as Maris Piper or King
  Edward, peeled
2 tablespoons **olive oil**
1 teaspoon **sea salt**
2 **rosemary** sprigs (optional)

Cut the potatoes into even-sized pieces, about 3.5 cm (1½ inches) across. Cook in a saucepan of lightly salted boiling water for 7 minutes, then drain in a colander and leave to steam dry for 3 minutes.

Shake the colander to rough up the edges of the potatoes – this helps make them extra crispy. Place the potatoes in a bowl, add the olive oil, salt and rosemary, if using, and turn to coat in the oil.

Cook in a preheated air fryer at 200°C (400°F) for 20 minutes, turning halfway through, then shaking the basket once more, until the potatoes are golden and crispy. Serve immediately.

For Hasselback potatoes, you will need 12 new potatoes, about 5–7 cm (2–3 inches) long. Make multiple parallel cuts down into each potato, like slicing a loaf of bread, but making sure you don't cut all the way through. Place in a bowl and drizzle over 2 teaspoons of olive oil, then add ½ teaspoon of salt and some pepper. Mix well to coat in the oil. Cook, cut sides up, in a preheated air fryer at 180°C (350°F) for 20–25 minutes, until crispy and cooked through.

honey & thyme roasted roots

Serves **3–4**
Preparation time **5 minutes**
Cooking time **18 minutes**

325 g (11 oz) **parsnips**,
  peeled and cut into 3.5 cm
  (1 ½ inch) pieces
325 g (11 oz) **Chantenay
  carrots**, halved if large
1 tablespoon **olive oil**
2 tablespoons **honey**
2 **thyme sprigs**
salt and **pepper**

Place the parsnips and carrots in a bowl, add the oil, honey and thyme, season to taste and stir well to coat.

Cook in a preheated air fryer at 180°C (350°F) for 15–18 minutes, turning halfway through and brushing with any remaining mixture in the bowl, until caramelized and tender. Serve immediately.

For marmalade & tarragon roasted carrots,

place 25 g (1 oz) of butter and 1 tablespoon of orange marmalade in an ovenproof dish and place in a preheated air fryer at 180°C (350°F) for 2 minutes to melt together. Toss in 625 g (1 ¼ lb) of Chantenay carrots, halved if large, and turn to coat. Cook for 15–18 minutes, stirring halfway through, until glazed and tender. Stir in 1 tablespoon of chopped tarragon and season to taste before serving.

cheesy gratin potatoes

Serves **4**

Preparation time **15 minutes**

Cooking time **38 minutes**

butter, for greasing

450 g (14½ oz) **potatoes**,
  peeled

150 ml (¼ pint) **double cream**

150 ml (¼ pint) **milk**

2 **garlic cloves**, crushed

pinch of grated **nutmeg**

25 g (1 oz) **Gruyère** or **mature
  Cheddar cheese**, grated

salt and **pepper**

Grease a 17 cm (6½ inch) square ovenproof dish. Slice the potatoes to about 2.5 mm (⅛ inch) thick and layer them in the dish.

Place the cream, milk, garlic, nutmeg and salt and pepper in a saucepan over a medium heat and bring to the boil. Pour over the potatoes in the dish. Place the dish in a preheated air fryer and cook at 150°C (300°F) for 30 minutes, stirring gently every 10 minutes, until tender.

Sprinkle over the cheese, increase the temperature to 180°C (350°F) and cook for a further 4–5 minutes, until the topping is golden. Allow to stand for a few minutes for the cream to thicken before serving.

For pancetta, mustard & thyme gratin, place 150 g (5 oz) of cubed pancetta in a baking tin, place the tin in a preheated air fryer and cook at 180°C (350°F) for 3–4 minutes, stirring once, until crispy. Drain on kitchen paper. Prepare the potatoes as above and layer in an ovenproof dish with the pancetta. Mix 1 tablespoon of wholegrain mustard with the cream, milk and garlic, omitting the nutmeg, and stir in 2 teaspoons of chopped thyme leaves. Heat as above, then pour over the potatoes and cook as above, omitting the cheese.

crispy sesame noodles

Serves **2–3**
Preparation time **2 minutes**
Cooking time **16 minutes**

125 g (4 oz) **dried medium egg noodles**
2 teaspoons **sesame oil**
2 teaspoons grated **fresh root ginger**
½ teaspoon **salt**
150 g (5 oz) **bean sprouts**
4 **spring onions**, thinly sliced
2 teaspoons toasted **sesame seeds**

Cook the noodles in a saucepan of boiling water according to the packet instructions, until just tender, then drain well.

Place the noodles in a bowl, add the oil, ginger and salt and toss well. Cook on a piece of pierced nonstick baking paper in a preheated air fryer at 190°C (375°F) for 7 minutes, until starting to crisp. Add the bean sprouts, stir well and cook for a further 5 minutes, until all the noodles are crispy.

Serve immediately sprinkled with the spring onions and toasted sesame seeds.

For crispy chilli noodles, toss the cooked noodles in 2 teaspoons of chilli oil, 1 teaspoon of soy sauce, 2 teaspoons of grated fresh root ginger and 1 crushed garlic clove. Cook as above. Serve sprinkled with the spring onions, sesame seeds and a few slices of fresh red chilli.

baked sweet potatoes

Serves **4**

Preparation time **4 minutes**

Cooking time **40 minutes**

4 **sweet potatoes**, scrubbed

1 tablespoon **olive oil**

2 teaspoons **sea salt**, plus extra to serve

1 teaspoon freshly ground **black pepper**, plus extra to serve

butter or **vegan butter**, to serve

Prick the sweet potatoes all over with a fork, rub with the oil and sprinkle over the sea salt and black pepper.

Cook them slightly apart in a preheated air fryer at 190°C (375°F) for 35–40 minutes, turning halfway through, until tender. The cooking time may vary, depending on the size of your potatoes. Slice open the sweet potatoes and serve with butter and extra salt and pepper.

For cheesy baked potatoes, prick 4 baking potatoes all over with a fork, rub with the oil, salt and pepper, then cook as above for 40–50 minutes, depending on their size, turning over once, until the skin is crispy and the potatoes are tender. Slice open the potatoes and top each with a knob of butter and a handful of grated Cheddar cheese.

balsamic asparagus & broccoli

Serves **2–3**
Preparation time **4 minutes**
Cooking time **9 minutes**

200 g (7 oz) **asparagus spears**, woody stems removed
150 g (5 oz) **Tenderstem broccoli**, stalks trimmed
1 teaspoon **olive oil**
1 teaspoon **balsamic vinegar**
salt and **pepper**
15 g (½ oz) **Parmesan cheese**, to serve

Place the asparagus spears and broccoli in a bowl, add the oil, vinegar and salt and pepper and toss well.

Cook the asparagus in a single layer in a preheated air fryer at 190°C (375°F) for 4 minutes, then turn the asparagus and add the broccoli. Cook for a further 4–5 minutes, until tender and starting to crisp.

Place in a serving dish and use a vegetable peeler to shave the Parmesan over the top. Serve immediately.

For crispy broccoli florets, toss 375 g (12 oz) of small broccoli florets in 2 tablespoons of olive oil and season with ½ teaspoon of salt, a good grind of black pepper and a pinch of dried chilli flakes. Sprinkle over 4 tablespoons of grated Pecorino or Parmesan cheese. Cook in a preheated air fryer at 190°C (375°F) for 5–6 minutes, shaking the basket a couple of times, until crispy.

crispy rosemary & garlic wedges

Serves **2**
Preparation time **5 minutes**
Cooking time **15 minutes**

2 **baking potatoes**, scrubbed
2 teaspoons **olive oil**
½ teaspoon **paprika**
1 tablespoon chopped
   rosemary
2 **garlic cloves**, crushed
salt and **pepper**

Cut each potato into 8 wedges. Place the remaining ingredients in a bowl, add the wedges and toss to coat.

Cook in a single layer in a preheated air fryer at 190°C (375°F) for 10 minutes. Turn the wedges and cook for a further 5 minutes, until crispy and tender. Serve immediately.

For spicy potato wedges, toss the potato wedges in the olive oil, 2 teaspoons of paprika, 1 teaspoon each of ground cumin and dried mixed herbs, ¼ teaspoon of cayenne pepper and ½ teaspoon of salt. Toss well to coat in the herbs and spices and cook as above.

vegetable egg 'fried' rice

Serves **2–3**
Preparation time **5 minutes**
Cooking time **19 minutes**

1 teaspoon **sunflower oil**
1 **carrot**, finely diced
½ small **red pepper**, cored, deseeded and chopped
1 head of **pak choi**, white stalks sliced and leaves halved if large
250 g (8 oz) cooked **long-grain rice**
2 **spring onions**, chopped
1 teaspoon **toasted sesame oil**
1 large **egg**, beaten
75 g (3 oz) **frozen peas**, defrosted
1 tablespoon **light soy sauce**

Place the sunflower oil in a 20 cm (8 inch) round cake tin or ovenproof dish. Place in a preheated air fryer at 180°C (350°F) for 2 minutes to heat up. Add the carrot, red pepper and pak choi stalks, stir to coat in the oil, then cook for 4 minutes, stirring halfway through.

Meanwhile, place the rice and spring onions in a bowl, add the sesame oil and stir to coat. Add the rice to the vegetables and stir well, then cook for a further 10 minutes, stirring halfway through.

Add the egg to the top of the rice and cook for 3 minutes until just set. Break up the egg with a fork, stir in the peas, pak choi leaves and soy sauce, then cook for a further 2 minutes. Serve immediately.

For prawn rice with peas, place 1 teaspoon each of sunflower and sesame oil in the tin and heat as above. Stir in 1 crushed garlic clove, 2 teaspoons of grated fresh root ginger, ½ deseeded and chopped red chilli, the cooked long-grain rice and 2 chopped spring onions. Cook for 10 minutes, stirring halfway through. Add the egg to the top of the rice and cook for 3 minutes, then break up the egg with a fork and stir in 75 g (3 oz) of defrosted frozen peas, 250 g (8 oz) of small cooked peeled prawns and the light soy sauce. Cook for a further 2–3 minutes.

spicy maple-glazed squash

Serves **2–3**
Preparation time **10 minutes**
Cooking time **15 minutes**

1 tablespoon **olive oil**
2 tablespoons **maple syrup**
1 **red chilli**, deseeded and
    finely chopped
2 tablespoons chopped
    rosemary
1 teaspoon **smoked paprika**
350 g (11½ oz) **butternut
    squash**, peeled, deseeded
    and cut into 1 cm (½ inch)
    thick wedges
salt and **pepper**

Place the oil, maple syrup, chilli, rosemary and paprika
in a large bowl and season well. Add the squash and turn
to coat.

Cook in a single layer in a preheated air fryer at 180°C
(350°F) for 15 minutes, until caramelized and tender,
turning halfway through and spooning over any remaining
mixture in the bowl. Serve immediately.

For cumin-roasted butternut with feta, toss the
butternut squash wedges with the olive oil and 1 tablespoon
of cumin seeds and season to taste. Cook as above, then
transfer to a serving plate and scatter over 125 g (4 oz)
of crumbled feta cheese, 50 g (2 oz) of toasted chopped
hazelnuts and 2 tablespoons of chopped flat leaf parsley.

perfect chips

Serves **4**

Preparation time **5 minutes,
plus chilling**

Cooking time **20 minutes**

4 large **floury potatoes**,
such as Maris Piper or King
Edward, peeled

2 teaspoons **olive oil**

½ teaspoon **salt**

Cut the potatoes into 1.5 cm (¾ inch) thick chips. Place in a bowl and cover with cold water, then chill in the refrigerator for 30 minutes.

Drain the chips and pat dry, then place in a bowl and toss with the oil and salt.

Cook in a preheated air fryer at 160°C (325°F) for 12 minutes, shaking halfway through. Increase the temperature to 200°C (400°F) and cook for a further 8 minutes, shaking occasionally, until golden and crisp. Do not overfill the air fryer or the chips won't cook evenly – you may need to do this in 2 batches. If so, return all the chips to the air fryer at the end and cook for a further 2 minutes. Serve immediately.

For truffle & Parmesan chips, prepare the potatoes as above and toss in 2 teaspoons of truffle oil. Cook as above, then tip into a warmed serving dish. Drizzle over a little more truffle oil and sprinkle with 50 g (2 oz) of grated Parmesan cheese. Toss together and serve immediately.

cauliflower bites with chilli sauce

Serves **4–6**
Preparation time **10 minutes**
Cooking time **15 minutes**

1 small **cauliflower**, about
    325 g (11 oz)
1 teaspoon **paprika**
1 teaspoon **garlic powder**
½ teaspoon **onion powder**
50 g (2 oz) **plain flour**
½ teaspoon **salt**
125 ml (4 fl oz) **buttermilk**
75 g (3 oz) **panko**
    breadcrumbs
sunflower oil, for spritzing
1 tablespoon toasted **sesame
    seeds**
2 **spring onions**, thinly sliced

Chilli sauce
3 tablespoons **sriracha
    chilli sauce**
3 tablespoons **sweet
    chilli sauce**
juice of **1 lime**
1 tablespoon **honey**

Cut the cauliflower into bite-sized florets of roughly the same size so they cook evenly. Mix the paprika, garlic powder and onion powder with the flour and salt in a large bowl and stir in the buttermilk to make a thick, smooth batter. Add the cauliflower florets and stir well so they are evenly coated.

Place the breadcrumbs in a shallow bowl, add the cauliflower, a few florets at a time, and toss to coat. Place in a preheated air fryer, spritz with oil and cook at 190°C (375°F) for 15 minutes, shaking halfway through, until just tender.

Meanwhile, gently heat all the sauce ingredients together in a small saucepan until hot and well combined. Place the cauliflower in a serving bowl, pour over the sauce and toss to coat. Scatter over the toasted sesame seeds and spring onions and serve immediately.

For hot & sweet cauliflower bites, prepare the florets as above and place in a large bowl. Add 2 teaspoons of sriracha sauce, 2 teaspoons of soy sauce, 2 teaspoons of maple syrup or honey and 2 teaspoons of olive oil. Toss together, then cook in a preheated air fryer at 180°C (350°F) for 12–14 minutes, shaking the basket a couple of times during cooking.

tear & share bread rolls

Makes **9**

Preparation time **25 minutes, plus proving**

Cooking time **20 minutes**

50 g (2 oz) **butter**, melted, plus extra for greasing and brushing

300 g (10 oz) **strong white bread flour**, plus extra for dusting

½ teaspoon **salt**

7 g (¼ oz) **fast-action dried yeast**

1 tablespoon **caster sugar**

200 ml (7 fl oz) lukewarm **milk**

1 **egg**, beaten

2 tablespoons **mixed seeds**

Grease a 20 cm (8 inch) springform cake tin. Place the flour, salt, yeast and sugar in a bowl and add the milk. Bring together until the mixture forms a rough dough, then knead on a lightly floured surface for 10–15 minutes, until smooth and elastic.

Add the melted butter and knead until it has been incorporated. Transfer to a lightly greased bowl, cover with a damp clean tea towel and leave to prove in a warm place for about 45–60 minutes, until doubled in size.

Knead the dough again on a lightly floured surface for 2 minutes, then divide into 9 equal ball shapes. Place 6 of the dough balls around the edge of the prepared tin, leaving a small space between them, then arrange the remaining 3 in the middle. Cover with a damp tea towel and leave to prove in a warm place for 30 minutes.

Brush the tops of the rolls with a little beaten egg, then sprinkle over the seeds. Place the tin in a preheated air fryer and cook at 160°C (325°F) for 15 minutes. Remove the tin, carefully turn the bread rolls over and return to the air fryer. Cook for a further 4–5 minutes, until golden.

Place the rolls on a wire rack and brush with melted butter.

For garlic tear & share, add 1 teaspoon of garlic powder to the dough mixture and omit the seeds from the top of the bread. While the bread is cooking, mix 25 g (1 oz) of softened butter with 2 tablespoons of finely chopped parsley. When the buns are cooked, brush the tops and sides with the parsley butter and serve warm.

sweet potato fries

Makes **2–3**
Preparation time **5 minutes**
Cooking time **26 minutes**

2 **sweet potatoes**, scrubbed
2 teaspoons **olive oil**
½ teaspoon **sea salt**
4 teaspoons **cornmeal** or
  polenta
ketchup, to serve

Cut the sweet potatoes into 1 cm (½ inch) thick fries.
Rinse in cold water, then pat dry on kitchen paper or
in a clean tea towel.

Place in a bowl, drizzle over the oil and sprinkle with
the salt and cornmeal or polenta. Toss the fries until
evenly coated.

Cook half the fries in a single layer in a preheated air
fryer at 190°C (375°F) for 10–12 minutes, shaking once.
Repeat with the remaining fries, then return them all to
the basket and cook for 2 minutes until hot and crispy.
Serve immediately with ketchup.

For garlic & herb sweet potato fries, prepare the
sweet potatoes as above and drizzle with the oil. Mix the
cornmeal or polenta with 1 teaspoon of garlic powder,
2 teaspoons of dried mixed herbs, ½ teaspoon of sea
salt and a good grind of black pepper. Toss the fries in
the mixture and cook as above.

sweet things

baked lemon curd cheesecake

Serves **8**

Preparation time **15 minutes, plus chilling**

Cooking time **40 minutes**

50 g (2 oz) **butter**, plus extra for greasing

200 g (7 oz) **ginger biscuits**, crushed

400 g (13 oz) **cream cheese**

75 g (3 oz) **caster sugar**

250 g (8 oz) **lemon curd**

100 ml (3½ fl oz) **soured cream**

3 **eggs**

50 g (2 oz) **plain flour**

lemon zest, to decorate

Grease and line the base of an 18 cm (7 inch) springform cake tin with nonstick baking paper. Melt the butter in a saucepan, then stir in the crushed biscuits and press into the base of the tin in an even layer. Chill in the refrigerator while you make the filling.

Place the cream cheese, sugar and 200 g (7 oz) of the lemon curd in a bowl and whisk until smooth. Whisk in the soured cream and eggs, then fold in the flour and pour the mixture over the biscuit base.

Cook in a preheated air fryer at 150°C (300°F) for 35–40 minutes, until the sides are set but the middle is still slightly wobbly. Cover the top with foil if it becomes too brown. Allow to cool at room temperature, then chill in the refrigerator for at least 4 hours or overnight.

Spread the top with the reserved lemon curd and decorate with lemon zest just before serving.

For orange curd & chocolate cheesecake, grease and line the tin as above. Make the base by substituting the ginger biscuits with 200 g (7 oz) of dark chocolate digestive biscuits. Make the filling as above, but replace the lemon curd with 200 g (7 oz) of orange curd. When ready to serve, spread the top of the cheesecake with 50 g (2 oz) of orange curd and grate over some dark chocolate to decorate.

chocolate orange fondant puds

Serves **4**

Preparation time **10 minutes**

Cooking time **7 minutes**

75 g (3 oz) **unsalted butter**, softened, plus extra for greasing

150 g (5 oz) **dark chocolate** (about 70% cocoa solids), chopped

2 teaspoons grated **orange zest**, plus extra to decorate

25 g (1 oz) **light soft brown sugar**

3 **eggs**

25 g (1 oz) **plain flour**, sifted

2 teaspoons **orange extract** or liqueur

vanilla ice cream or **crème fraîche**, to serve

Grease 4 metal pudding tins or ramekins, about 150 ml (¼ pint) capacity each. Place the chocolate and orange zest in a bowl set over a saucepan of simmering water. Once melted, stir until smooth, then allow to cool slightly.

Place the butter, sugar, eggs, flour and orange extract in a food processor and blend to make a smooth batter. Add the melted chocolate and blend again until well combined.

Divide the mixture between the prepared tins and place the tins in a preheated air fryer. Cook at 190°C (375°F) for 7 minutes. The outsides will be cooked but the centres will still be molten. Serve immediately with vanilla ice cream or crème fraîche, decorated with orange zest.

For chocolate & salted caramel fondants, prepare the fondants as above, omitting the orange zest and extract. Divide half the mixture between the 4 prepared tins, then add 1 teaspoon of salted caramel sauce to the middle of each and spoon the remaining mixture over the top. Cook as above and serve with salted caramel ice cream.

fruity olive oil scones

Makes **6**
Preparation time **10 minutes**
Cooking time **10 minutes**

225 g (7½ oz) **self-raising
  flour**, plus extra for dusting
1 teaspoon **baking powder**
25 g (1 oz) **caster sugar**
50 g (2 oz) **mixed dried fruit**
1 **egg**
50 ml (2 fl oz) **mild olive oil**
5 tablespoons **milk**, plus extra
  for brushing

To serve
strawberry jam
clotted cream

Place the flour, baking powder, sugar and dried fruit in a large bowl. Stir well to combine.

Crack the egg into a measuring jug, then beat in the olive oil and milk. Stir the mixture into the flour and mix to a soft, sticky dough. Turn out on to a lightly floured surface, knead lightly and roll out to about 2.5 cm (1 inch) thick.

Cut into 6 rounds with a fluted 6 cm (2½ inch) cutter, using the trimmings as necessary to make more scones. Place on a piece of pierced nonstick baking paper in a preheated air fryer, brush the tops of the scones with a little extra milk and cook at 180°C (350°F) for 5 minutes.

Turn the scones over and cook for a further 5 minutes, or until well risen and golden brown. Transfer to a wire rack to cool. To serve, split the scones and serve with strawberry jam and a good dollop of clotted cream.

For blueberry & lemon scones, sift the flour and baking powder into a bowl and rub in 50 g (2 oz) of cubed butter until the mixture resembles fine breadcrumbs. Stir in the caster sugar and 50 g (2 oz) of blueberries. Whisk the milk with 1 tablespoon of lemon curd and stir into the mixture to make a soft dough. Knead and roll out as above and cut into 6 rounds. Brush the tops with a little milk and cook as above. Serve warm with clotted cream and a little extra lemon curd.

bananas with miso caramel sauce

Serves **2**

Preparation time **10 minutes**

Cooking time **14 minutes**

25 g (1 oz) **unsalted butter**

25 g (1 oz) **light soft brown sugar**

1 tablespoon **golden syrup**

3 tablespoons **double cream**

1–2 teaspoons **white miso paste**

50 g (2 oz) **plain flour**

125 ml (4 fl oz) **cold water**

25 g (1 oz) **panko breadcrumbs**

2 **bananas**, cut in half

sunflower oil, for spritzing

ice cream, to serve

Place the butter, sugar and syrup in a small saucepan. Melt over a gentle heat, stirring until the sugar has dissolved. Add the cream and miso paste and boil for 3–4 minutes, until thickened. Allow to cool slightly.

Meanwhile, place the flour in a bowl and gradually add the measured water, whisking so there are no lumps, until you have a thick batter the consistency of double cream.

Place the breadcrumbs in a shallow bowl, dunk each banana half in the batter to fully coat, then roll in the breadcrumbs.

Spritz generously with oil, then cook in a preheated air fryer at 200°C (400°F) for 6–8 minutes, turning once, until golden and crispy. Serve immediately with a scoop of ice cream topped with the warm caramel sauce.

For coconut bananas, mix 25 g (1 oz) of fine dried breadcrumbs and 25 g (1 oz) of desiccated coconut in a bowl. Prepare the bananas and batter as above, then dip the bananas in the batter, followed by the coconut crumb. Cook as above, then serve with chocolate ice cream.

cappuccino cupcakes

Makes **4**

Preparation time **10 minutes, plus cooling**

Cooking time **15 minutes**

50 g (2 oz) **self-raising flour**

1 tablespoon **cocoa powde**r, sifted, plus extra for dusting

50 g (2 oz) **unsalted butter**, softened

50 g (2 oz) **caster sugar**

1 **egg**, beaten

2 teaspoons **instant coffee**, dissolved in 1 tablespoon **boiling water**

Vanilla buttercream

50 g (2 oz) **unsalted butter**, softened

150 g (5 oz) **icing sugar**, sifted

½ teaspoon **vanilla extract**

Line 4 small cake tins or ramekins with paper muffin cases. Place all the cake ingredients in a bowl and beat with an electric whisk until combined.

Divide the mixture between the paper cases and level the tops. Place the tins in a preheated air fryer and cook at 160°C (325°F) for 13–15 minutes, until springy to the touch. Allow to cool for a few minutes, then transfer to a wire rack to cool completely.

Place the butter for the icing in a bowl and gradually beat in the icing sugar a little at a time. Once all the sugar has been added, add the vanilla and beat together. Pipe or spoon the buttercream on the cakes and decorate with a dusting of cocoa powder.

For coffee & walnut cupcakes, prepare the cake mixture as above, omitting the cocoa powder and stirring in 25 g (1 oz) of chopped walnuts. Cook as above. To make the buttercream, beat together the butter and icing sugar as above. Dissolve 1 teaspoon of instant coffee in 2 teaspoons of boiling water, allow to cool, then beat into the buttercream. Pipe or spoon on the cakes, then top each with half a walnut.

churros with chilli-chocolate sauce

Makes **16**

Preparation time **10 minutes, plus cooling**

Cooking time **24 minutes**

125 g (4 oz) **self-raising flour**
pinch of **salt**
25 g (1 oz) **butter**
150 ml (¼ pint) **boiling water**
½ teaspoon **vanilla extract**
25 g (1 oz) **caster sugar**
½ teaspoon **ground cinnamon**
sunflower oil, for spritzing

Dipping sauce
100 g (3½ oz) **dark chocolate with chilli** or **dark chocolate and a pinch of chilli flakes**, broken into small pieces
50 ml (2 fl oz) **double cream**
2 teaspoons **golden syrup**

Place the flour and salt in a bowl, stir and make a well in the centre. Melt the butter in a jug in the microwave, then pour in the measured water and add the vanilla. Pour into the well and stir to make a lump-free dough. Leave to cool for about 10 minutes.

Meanwhile, mix together the sugar and cinnamon in a shallow bowl.

Transfer the dough to a piping bag fitted with a star-shaped nozzle. Pipe about 8 churros, 10 cm (4 inches) long, on to a piece of pierced nonstick baking paper, cutting the dough with scissors. Place the paper in a preheated air fryer at 190°C (375°F), spritz with oil and cook for 10 minutes, until browned. Turn the churros over and cook for a further 2 minutes, then toss in the cinnamon sugar. Repeat with the remaining dough.

Meanwhile, place all the sauce ingredients in a small saucepan and cook over a gentle heat, stirring, until melted. Keep warm. Serve the hot churros with the hot chocolate sauce for dipping.

For salted caramel dipping sauce, to replace the chilli-chocolate sauce, place 100 g (3½ oz) of unsalted butter in a saucepan with 75 g (3 oz) of light soft brown sugar, 75 ml (3 fl oz) of golden syrup and 1 teaspoon of vanilla extract. Bring to the boil over a medium heat, stirring continuously. Pour in 150 ml (¼ pint) of double cream and ½ teaspoon of coarse sea salt. Boil for 5 minutes, stirring occasionally, until thickened. Transfer to a bowl and serve with the churros.

cocoa swirl meringues

Makes **4**

Preparation time **10 minutes, plus cooling**

Cooking time **40 minutes**

2 **egg whites**

100 g (3½ oz) **caster sugar**

½ teaspoon **cornflour**

½ teaspoon **white wine vinegar**

1 teaspoon **cocoa powder**, plus extra for dusting

150 ml (¼ pint) **double cream**

1 teaspoon **vanilla extract**

125 g (4 oz) **strawberries**, hulled and sliced

Place the egg whites in a clean mixing bowl and use an electric whisk to beat until they form stiff peaks. Add the sugar a tablespoon at a time, whisking well after each addition, until the mixture is smooth, thick and glossy. Whisk in the cornflour and vinegar.

Sift the cocoa powder over the top and use a metal spoon to fold it over a few times until the mixture is streaked.

Place 4 heaped tablespoons of the mixture, spaced a little apart, on a piece of pierced nonstick baking paper. Place the paper in a preheated air fryer and cook at 120°C (250°F) for 35–40 minutes, until the outsides are dry and firm. Allow to cool in the air fryer.

Whisk the cream with the vanilla until thick. Spoon on to the meringues, top with the strawberries and dust with a little cocoa powder. Serve immediately.

For pistachio meringues with rosewater cream & raspberries, prepare the meringues as above, omitting the cocoa powder but stirring in 25 g (1 oz) of chopped pistachios. Cook as above and allow to cool. Whisk the double cream with 1 teaspoon of rosewater and 1 teaspoon of icing sugar, until thick. Spoon on to the cooled meringues, top with 125 g (4 oz) of raspberries and decorate with a few extra chopped pistachios.

apple & cinnamon crisps

Serves **2**
Preparation time **5 minutes**
Cooking time **24 minutes**

2 **dessert apples**
1 teaspoon **ground cinnamon**

Cut the apples into 2.5 mm ($\frac{1}{8}$ inch) thick slices using a mandolin or sharp knife and remove any seeds.

Place in a bowl, sprinkle over the cinnamon and toss well to coat evenly. Cook half the slices in a single layer in a preheated air fryer at 150°C (300°F) for 10–12 minutes, turning halfway through, until crisp.

Transfer to a wire rack to cool and continue crisping, then repeat with the remaining apple slices. Store any leftover crisps in an airtight container for 1–2 days.

For apple rings with raisins, honey & cinnamon,
core the apples and cut each into 4 thick rings. Mix 15 g (½ oz) of melted butter with 2 tablespoons of honey, ½ teaspoon of ground cinnamon and 4 tablespoons of raisins or sultanas. Place the apple rings in an ovenproof dish and spoon over the raisin mixture. Place the dish in a preheated air fryer and cook at 190°C (375°F) for 10 minutes, turning the rings halfway through, until softened and starting to caramelize. Divide between 2 plates and spoon over the juices from the dish. Serve with a scoop of vanilla ice cream.

blueberry & lemon muffins

Makes **4**

Preparation time **10 minutes, plus cooling**

Cooking time **15 minutes**

3 tablespoons **sunflower** or **light olive oil**

1 **egg**

3 tablespoons **milk**

finely grated zest of **1 lemon**

1 tablespoon **lemon juice**

125 g (4 oz) **plain flour**

1 teaspoon **baking powder**

½ teaspoon **salt**

3 tablespoons **caster sugar**

75 g (3 oz) **blueberries**, plus extra to decorate

Lemon icing

4 tablespoons **icing sugar**

1 teaspoon finely grated **lemon zest**, plus extra to decorate

1 teaspoon **lemon juice**

Line 4 small cake tins or ramekins with paper muffin cases. In a jug, whisk together the oil, egg, milk, lemon zest and juice.

Stir the flour, baking powder, salt and sugar together in a bowl, then stir the wet ingredients into the dry ingredients until just combined. Stir in the blueberries.

Divide the mixture between the cases and place the tins in a preheated air fryer. Cook at 160°C (325°F) for 14–15 minutes, until springy to the touch. Allow to cool on a wire rack.

Make the icing by mixing all the ingredients together, then spoon over the cooled muffins and top with some extra blueberries and lemon zest.

For raspberry, lemon & white chocolate muffins,

prepare the muffins as above, substituting the blueberries the 75 g (3 oz) of raspberries and stirring in 1 tablespoon of white chocolate chunks at the same time. Cook and ice as above, topping each with a raspberry.

glazed ring & mini doughnuts

Makes **6 ring doughnuts and 6 mini doughnuts**
Preparation time **20 minutes, plus proving and cooling**
Cooking time **10 minutes**

275 g (9 oz) **plain flour**, plus extra for dusting
50 g (2 oz) **caster sugar**
½ teaspoon **salt**
7 g (¼ oz) **fast-action dried yeast**
125 ml (4 fl oz) **milk**
50 g (2 oz) **butter**
1 **egg**, beaten
sunflower oil, for greasing and spritzing
125 g (4 oz) **icing sugar**
3–4 teaspoons **cold water**
sprinkles, **freeze-dried raspberries** and **freeze-dried raspberry powder**, to decorate

Place the flour, sugar, salt and yeast in a bowl. Place the milk and butter in a saucepan and heat until the butter has melted and the milk is lukewarm. Add the milk mixture and egg to the flour. Bring together until the mixture forms a rough dough, then knead on a lightly floured surface for 10 minutes, until smooth and elastic. Transfer to a lightly greased bowl, cover with a damp clean tea towel and leave to prove in a warm place for 1 hour, until doubled in size.

Knock back the dough and knead for 2 minutes. Roll out to 1 cm (½ inch) thick. Use a 9 cm (3½ inch) cookie cutter to cut out 6 rounds. Use a 4 cm (1¾ inch) cutter to cut out holes in the centres, keeping the cut-outs as mini doughnuts. Repeat with the trimmings. Place the doughnuts, spaced, on a baking sheet lined with nonstick baking paper. Cover with a damp tea towel and prove in a warm place for 30–45 minutes, until doubled in size.

Spritz the cooking plate in a preheated air fryer with oil and carefully place 3 ring doughnuts and 3 mini doughnuts on it. Cook at 180°C (350°F) for 4–5 minutes, until risen, puffed and golden brown. Transfer to a wire rack to cool, then repeat with the remaining doughnuts.

Sift the icing sugar into a bowl. Stir in enough water to make an icing that coats the back of a spoon. Dip the tops of the doughnuts in the icing, then sprinkle with decorations.

For cinnamon sugar doughnuts, prepare and cook the doughnuts as above. Mix together 200 g (7 oz) of caster sugar and 1 tablespoon of ground cinnamon in a bowl. Brush the warm doughnuts with 50 g (2 oz) of melted butter, then toss in the cinnamon sugar.

chocolate chip cookies

Makes **6**

Preparation time **10 minutes,
  plus chilling and cooling**

Cooking time **32 minutes**

50 g (2 oz) **light soft brown
  sugar**

50 g (2 oz) **granulated sugar**

75 g (3 oz) **butter**, softened

1 **egg yolk**

½ teaspoon **vanilla extract**

125 g (4 oz) **plain flour**

¼ teaspoon **salt**

½ teaspoon **baking powder**

75 g (3 oz) **dark chocolate
  chips**

Place the sugars and butter in a large mixing bowl. Beat together with an electric hand whisk until smooth and creamy. Add the egg yolk and vanilla extract and whisk until combined.

Sift in the flour, salt and baking powder and mix with a wooden spoon or spatula until all the ingredients are combined. Stir in the chocolate chips and bring the dough together. Roll the dough into 6 balls and flatten slightly. Chill in the refrigerator for at least 1 hour.

Place 3 cookies on a piece of pierced nonstick baking paper in a preheated air fryer and cook at 160°C (325°F) for 16 minutes, or until golden. Allow to cool in the air fryer for 5 minutes, then transfer to a wire rack to cool completely. Repeat with the remaining cookies.

For vegan peanut & chocolate cookies, use an electric whisk to beat 50 g (2 oz) of vegan baking spread in a bowl with 75 g (3 oz) of caster sugar and ½ teaspoon of vanilla extract. Whisk in 50 g (2 oz) of crunchy peanut butter until smooth. Stir in 75 g (3 oz) of self-raising flour and 50 g (2 oz) of vegan dark chocolate chunks. Roll the mixture into 8 balls and flatten slightly. Cook 4 at a time as above for 10 minutes. Allow to cool for 5–6 minutes in the air fryer, then transfer to a wire rack to cool completely.

passion fruit self-saucing pudding

Serves **4**

Preparation time **10 minutes**

Cooking time **45 minutes**

50 g (2 oz) **butter**, softened,
   plus extra for greasing
5 ripe **passion fruits**, halved
finely grated zest and juice of
   1 **lemon**
100 g (3½ oz) **caster sugar**
2 **eggs**, separated
50 g (2 oz) **self-raising flour**
175 ml (6 fl oz) **milk**
icing sugar, for dusting

Grease a 20 cm (8 inch) ovenproof dish or 1 litre (1¾ pint) soufflé dish. Scoop the flesh and seeds from the passion fruits into a jug, add the lemon juice and whisk together – you should have about 150 ml (¼ pint).

Put the butter, sugar and lemon zest in a bowl. Using an electric whisk, beat until fluffy, then whisk in the egg yolks a little at a time. Whisk in the flour a little at a time, alternating it with the passion fruit, then whisk in the milk. Wash the beaters, then whisk the egg whites in a clean bowl until they form stiff peaks. Gently fold into the passion fruit mixture, then pour into the prepared dish.

Place the dish in a preheated air fryer and cook at 150°C (300°F) for 45 minutes, covering the top with foil after 20 minutes, removing the plate or basket if needed. The pudding should be firm with a slight wobble. Leave to stand for 3–4 minutes, then serve dusted with icing sugar.

For individual passion fruit puddings, grease 4 nonstick metal pudding tins or ramekins, about 150 ml (¼ pint) capacity each, with butter. Place the pulp and seeds of 4 passion fruits in a saucepan with 2 tablespoons of caster sugar and simmer for 4–5 minutes, until syrupy. Push the pulp of 2 passion fruits through a sieve, discarding the seeds. Whizz 100 g (3½ oz) of butter, 100 g (3½ oz) of caster sugar and the grated rind of 1 lemon in a food processor until pale and fluffy. Mix in 1 egg, followed by another egg, then the passion fruit juice. Add 100 g (3½ oz) of self-raising flour and pulse until smooth. Divide between the prepared tins and cook in a preheated air fryer at 150°C (300°F) for 18–20 minutes, until risen and firm. Turn out and pour over the syrup to serve.

sticky toffee puddings

Serves **4**
Preparation time **10 minutes**
Cooking time **20 minutes**

75 g (3 oz) **unsalted butter**,
softened, plus extra for
greasing
75 g (3 oz) **pitted dates**,
roughly chopped
½ teaspoon **bicarbonate of
soda**
4 tablespoons **boiling water**
100 g (3½ oz) **light soft brown
sugar**
½ teaspoon **vanilla extract**
1 **egg**, beaten
75 g (3 oz) **self-raising flour**
vanilla ice cream, to serve

Sticky toffee sauce
100 g (3½ oz) **light soft brown
sugar**
50 g (2 oz) **butter**
2 tablespoons **double cream**
1 teaspoon **treacle**

Grease 4 metal pudding tins or ramekins, about 150 ml
(¼ pint) capacity each. Line the bases with a piece of
nonstick baking paper. Place the dates in a bowl, add the
bicarbonate of soda, pour over the measured water and
stir well. Set aside.

Whisk the butter and sugar together until light and fluffy,
then beat in the vanilla and egg, a little at a time. Fold in
the flour. Mash the date mixture with a fork and stir into
the mixture, then spoon into the prepared tins. Place the
tins in a preheated air fryer and cook at 150°C (300°F)
for 18–20 minutes, until risen and firm.

Meanwhile, place all the sauce ingredients in a small
saucepan and heat gently, stirring occasionally, until the
sugar has dissolved.

Turn the puddings out on to small plates and pour the
sauce over them. Serve immediately with a scoop of
vanilla ice cream.

For sticky ginger & date puddings, prepare the sponge
mixture as above, adding 1 piece of stem ginger, finely
chopped. To make the sauce, replace the treacle with
1 teaspoon of ginger syrup from the jar.

chocolate brownies

Makes **16**
Preparation time **10 minutes**
Cooking time **28 minutes**

125 g (4 oz) **unsalted butter**,
  cut into cubes, plus extra for
  greasing
75 g (3 oz) **cocoa powder**
2 **eggs**
225 g (7½ oz) **granulated
  sugar**
1 teaspoon **vanilla extract**
pinch of **salt**
50 g (2 oz) **plain flour**

Grease and line the base and sides of a 15 cm (6 inch) square cake tin, about 5 cm (2 inches) deep, with nonstick baking paper.

Place the butter and cocoa powder in a small saucepan over a low heat, stirring frequently until the butter has melted. Remove from the heat and leave to cool for 3–4 minutes.

Meanwhile, in a large bowl, whisk together the eggs, sugar, vanilla and salt with an electric whisk for about 2 minutes, until pale and thick. Add the cocoa and butter mixture and whisk to combine.

Sift the flour over the mixture and mix thoroughly, then pour into the prepared tin and level the top. Place the tin in a preheated air fryer and cook at 160°C (325°F) for 23–25 minutes, until just firm to the touch and a wooden cocktail stick inserted in the middle comes out with moist crumbs. Leave to cool in the tin before cutting into squares.

For sour cherry & white chocolate brownies, prepare the mixture as above, stirring in 50 g (2 oz) of dried sour cherries and 50 g (2 oz) of white chocolate chunks. Cook as above.

apple, blackberry & ginger crumble

Serves **4**

Preparation time **10 minutes**

Cooking time **22 minutes**

2 **Bramley apples**, peeled,
   cored and cut into 2 cm
   (¾ inch) chunks
1 tablespoon **caster sugar**
3 tablespoons **cold water**
125 g (4 oz) **blackberries**
custard, to serve

Crumble
125 g (4 oz) **plain flour**
75 g (3 oz) **butter**, cut into
   cubes
3 tablespoons **caster sugar**
4 tablespoons **porridge oats**
2 teaspoons **ground ginger**

Place the apples in an ovenproof dish, sprinkle over the sugar and add the measured water. Place the dish in a preheated air fryer and cook at 180°C (350°F) for 10 minutes, stirring halfway through, until the apples have softened slightly.

Meanwhile, make the crumble. In a large bowl, rub together the flour and butter until the mixture resembles fine breadcrumbs (or do this in a food processor). Stir in the sugar, oats and ginger.

Stir the blackberries into the apples, then sprinkle over the crumble topping. Cook for a further 10–12 minutes, until the topping is golden. Serve with custard.

For spiced apple & pecan crumble, place the apples in an ovenproof dish with 1 tablespoon of light soft brown sugar, ½ teaspoon each of ground mixed spice, ground ginger and ground cinnamon and 3 tablespoons of water. Cook as above. Make the crumble as above and stir in 25 g (1 oz) of chopped pecans. Spoon on top of the apples and cook as above.

peaches with amaretti & chocolate

Serves **4**
Preparation time **5 minutes**
Cooking time **10 minutes**

4 **peaches**, not too ripe, halved
  and pitted
100 g (3½ oz) **mascarpone
  cheese**
1 tablespoon **almond liqueur**
  or 1 teaspoon **almond
  extract**
5 **amaretti biscuits**
25 g (1 oz) **dark chocolate
  chunks**

Cook the peach halves, cut sides down, on a piece of pierced nonstick baking paper in a preheated air fryer at 180°C (350°F) for 6 minutes.

Meanwhile, mix the mascarpone with the almond liqueur, crumble in 4 of the biscuits and stir in the chocolate chunks.

Turn the peaches over and spoon some of the filling in the centre of each. Cook for a further 4 minutes, until the mascarpone has melted and the peaches are tender. Serve 2 peach halves per person, crumbling the remaining biscuit over the top.

For baked nectarines with maple syrup & cinnamon, cut 4 nectarines in half and remove the stones. In a bowl, mix together 1 tablespoon of maple syrup, 1 teaspoon of vanilla extract and 1 teaspoon of ground cinnamon. Place the nectarine halves on a piece of pierced nonstick baking paper in a preheated air fryer, drizzle over the maple syrup mixture and cook at 180°C (350°F) for 10–12 minutes, until tender. Serve with a spoonful of yogurt scattered with chopped hazelnuts.

crunchy ice cream balls

Serves **4**

Preparation time **10 minutes, plus freezing**

Cooking time **5 minutes**

4 scoops of **vanilla ice cream**

75 g (3 oz) **cinnamon crunch cereal** or cornflakes

2 **egg whites**

sunflower oil, for spritzing

Chocolate fudge sauce

200 ml (7 fl oz) **condensed milk**

25 g (1 oz) **unsalted butter**

75 g (3 oz) **dark chocolate chunks**

Line a baking sheet with nonstick baking paper. Place the ice cream balls on the tray and freeze for 2 hours.

Meanwhile, place the cereal in a food processor and pulse to a crumb. Place in a shallow dish. Whisk the egg whites until frothy.

Remove the ice cream from the freezer and dip the balls into the egg whites, then roll in the crumb mixture, coating completely. Reserve the remaining egg whites and crumbs. Freeze the ice cream balls for another hour, then dip again in the egg whites and coat again in the crumbs. Return to the freezer for at least 1 hour.

Make the chocolate fudge sauce when ready to serve. Place all the ingredients in a small saucepan over a low heat and stir until the chocolate and butter have melted.

Meanwhile, place the balls on a piece of pierced nonstick baking paper in a preheated air fryer, spritz with a little oil and cook at 200°C (400°F) for 2 minutes. Serve immediately with the warm fudge sauce.

For mint & chocolate ice cream balls, substitute the vanilla ice cream for with balls of mint and chocolate ice cream. Substitute the cinnamon crunch with 125 g (4 oz) of dark chocolate digestive biscuits, pulsed in a food processor to make a fine crumb. Prepare and cook as above. Serve with the warm fudge sauce.

olive oil, almond & orange cake

Serves **6–8**
Preparation time **10 minutes,**
   plus cooling
Cooking time **40 minutes**

125 ml (4 fl oz) **light olive oil,**
   plus extra for greasing
100 g (3½ oz) **plain flour**
1 teaspoon **baking powder**
pinch of **salt**
100 g (3½ oz) **golden caster**
   sugar
50 g (2 oz) **ground almonds**
finely grated zest and juice of
   1 orange
2 **eggs**, beaten

Orange syrup
grated zest and juice of
   1 large **orange**
50 g (2 oz) **caster sugar**
2 tablespoons **cold water**

Grease and line the base and sides of a 15 cm (6 inch) round cake tin, about 6 cm (2½ inches) deep, with nonstick baking paper. Sift the flour, baking powder and salt into a bowl, then stir in the sugar, almonds and orange zest.

Mix together the oil, orange juice and eggs, then pour into the flour mixture and stir to combine into a smooth batter. Pour into the prepared tin, place the tin in a preheated air fryer and cook at 150°C (300°F) for 35–40 minutes, until a cocktail stick inserted into the centre comes out clean. Cover the top with foil if it becomes too brown.

Meanwhile, put all the syrup ingredients in a saucepan, bring to the boil and simmer for 2–3 minutes.

Prick the top of the cake all over with a cocktail stick, then pour over the syrup and leave to cool in the tin for 10 minutes. Turn out on to a wire rack, remove the paper and leave to cool completely before serving.

For baked plums, to serve as an accompaniment, cut 6 plums in half and remove the stones. Mix 2 teaspoons of maple syrup with 1 teaspoon of finely grated orange zest and ½ teaspoon of ground cinnamon. Place the plums on a piece of pierced nonstick baking paper in a preheated air fryer, drizzle over the maple syrup mixture and cook at 180°C (350°F) for 6–8 minutes, until tender.

white choc & raspberry flapjacks

Makes **12**

Preparation time **15 minutes, plus cooling and setting**

Cooking time **14 minutes**

75 g (3 oz) **butter**, plus extra for greasing

2 tablespoons **golden syrup**

75 g (3 oz) **light soft brown sugar**

150 g (5 oz) **porridge oats**

75 g (3 oz) **white chocolate chunks**

50 g (2 oz) **raspberries**

Grease a 15 cm (6 inch) square cake tin. In a large saucepan, gently melt the golden syrup, butter and sugar over a low heat, stirring, until the sugar has dissolved.

Remove from the heat and stir in the oats, until well combined. Leave to cool for about 10 minutes.

Stir in two-thirds of the chocolate chunks and the raspberries, tip into the prepared tin and gently press down with the back of a spoon to even the top. Cover the tin with foil.

Place the tin in a preheated air fryer and cook at 180°C (350°F) for 10 minutes, then uncover and cook for a further 4 minutes, until golden on top. Leave to cool in the tin.

Melt the remaining white chocolate in a microwave or in a bowl set over a pan of simmering water. Remove the flapjacks from the tin, then use a teaspoon to drizzle the melted chocolate over the top. When the chocolate has set, cut the flapjacks into squares. Store any leftovers in an airtight container in the refrigerator, but they are best eaten the day they are made.

For chocolate & nut flapjacks, prepare the flapjack mixture as above, substituting the white chocolate chunks with 50 g (2 oz) of dark chocolate chunks, and the raspberries with 25 g (1 oz) of almonds and 25 g (1 oz) of Brazil nuts, cut into large chunks. Cook as above. When cool, remove from the tin and drizzle the top with 25 g (1 oz) of melted dark chocolate chunks.

index

glossary

UK	US
aubergine	eggplant
back bacon	Canadian bacon
bacon rasher	slice of bacon
baking paper	waxed paper
beetroot	beet
bicarbonate of soda	baking soda
biscuit	cookie
butty	sandwich
cake tin	baking tin, cake pan
caster sugar	superfine sugar
chickpea	garbanzo bean
chips	French fries
clingfilm	plastic wrap
cocktail stick	toothpick
coriander (fresh)	cilantro
cornflour	cornstarch
courgette	zucchini
crisps	chips
crumble (fruit)	crisp
dark chocolate	semi-sweet chocolate
desiccated coconut	shredded coconut
digestive biscuits	Graham crackers
double cream	heavy cream
dried chilli flakes	crushed red pepper flakes
fish fingers	fish sticks
flaked almonds	slivered almonds
foil	aluminum foil
gherkin	pickle
golden syrup	light corn syrup
grated	shredded
grill	broil
ground almonds	almond meal

UK	US
hob	stovetop
icing	frosting
icing sugar	confectioners' sugar
jam	preserves
joint, of meat	whole piece
jug	pitcher
king prawn	jumbo shrimp
kitchen paper	paper towel
marmalade	orange preserves
minced meat	ground meat
mixed spice	pie spice mix
muesli	granola
pak choi	bok choy
pepper (red, orange, yellow)	bell pepper
piping bag	pastry bag
plain flour	all-purpose flour
porridge oats	rolled oats
pudding	dessert
prawn	shrimp
rocket	arugula
salad leaves	greens
scone	biscuit
self-raising flour	self-rising flour
sirloin steak	strip steak
spring onion	scallion
stock	broth
streaky bacon	American bacon
tea towel	cloth kitchen towel
tomato purée	tomato paste
Tenderstem broccoli	long-stem broccoli
treacle	molasses
wholemeal	wholewheat

acknowledgements

Junior Editor: Louisa Johnson
Art Director: Jaz Bahra
Assistant Editor: Scarlet Furness
Copyeditor: Jo Smith
Photographer: William Shaw
Food Stylist: Denise Smart
Prop Stylist: Kim Sullivan
Production Controllers: Lucy Carter & Nic Jones
Picture Researchers: Giulia Hetherington & Jen Veall
Photography copyright © Octopus Publishing Group/William Shaw